DOUGLAS TILDEN: PORTRAIT

OF

A DEAF SCULPTOR

by

Mildred Albronda

T.J. PUBLISHERS, INC.
817 Silver Spring Avenue, 305-D   /   Silver Spring,
Maryland 20910

Printed in United States of America

ISBN #0-932666-03-5
Library of Congress Catalog No.: 80-65957

DOUGLAS TILDEN: PORTRAIT

OF

A DEAF SCULPTOR

CONTENTS

DEDICATED TO DOUGLAS TILDEN AND HIS CREDO

There is no other field in the struggle of life which can do more for the deaf than art, to secure recognition from the public and through this to bring them upon a common footing.

Indeed art can be a means of education.

Art will arouse the student's faculties to such a degree that he will speak out his soul with more success than is possible by any other means.

There is a beneficial connection between art and our language of image writing in the air.

A student may feel strongly, and yet have to brood over the chaos of his imaginings before he can shape them into a creation. This principle of vision is the same in literature, architecture, painting, sculpture, philosophy, and mathematics.

An average sign-making child has the faculty to a greater degree than an average hearing child of creating images on paper or in clay through memory.

No written or spoken sentence can reach the mind as swiftly and concentratedly as the thing seen . . . the language of images.

Drawing clearly has a proper place. . . . While learning to draw the student is led to higher and better things—to perceive grace, which we know as the principle of beauty.

Knowledge of the mechanical part of art . . . and acquaintance with its aims as an intellectual force will constitute an education: a boy will certainly be a better carpenter, a better engineer, and even a better editor or minister for having taken lessons in the art department.

Always bear in mind Aristotle's assertion that the most elemental intellectual quality is the power to recognize familiar [relationships in] objects.

The ideology underlying art and the sign-method are exactly the same. I see pictures mentally, and think in gesture.

Continually expressing myself in action is what puts me next to nature.

The ultimate object of art is to instruct, animate, and ennoble: for a deaf child who can only be an artisan, its object is to increase his efficiency and to render his life happier.

I beg that you deal tenderly with a gifted pupil . . . for his lot will be to see vividly, feel strongly, and suffer deeply . . . the pale vision seer, deaf, silent, and full of resentment against his fate may yet surmount his limitations, so that the delighted world will say, "The schools for the deaf are an honor to the land."

A capacity for understanding and enjoying beautiful things would form a precious possession for any deaf graduate and should be just as much his heritage as any hearing person's.

Society cannot exist in its fullest vigor unless the importance of art as a constructive force in human progress continues to be recognized. Art makes a state wealthy by showing that life in it is worth while. Art enriches life itself.

———— taken from Douglas Tilden's writings, 1892-1921

FOREWORD

A museum of art can be described as that place where collections of objects of enduring value are preserved, researched, and presented to the public. The basic differences between museums, besides their operating budgets and collections, come from the various methods employed to perform these functions. The presentation of the art is the activity that is the most apparent to the public and represents the museum's philosophy of how best to display and interpret its treasures. These methods of presentation cover a broad range of attitudes; there are those who prefer the direct confrontation of the art object without verbiage and devices standing in their way. Most museum directors and curators are sensitive to the needs and wishes of the visitor and attempt to fill the various gaps in understanding and appreciation with some type of interpretation. All visitors do not require the same materials and information to enrich their museum experience, and presenting a variety of sources in several forms results in reaching the greatest numbers.

At The Fine Arts Museums of San Francisco we make use of many of the traditional forms of art interpretation. Labels, catalogues, brochures, audio-visual presentations, lectures, recorded and printed tours are available. We also provide docent guides who present a more personal view of the collections. These volunteer docents are trained in art history, the museum collections, and teaching techniques, and are one of our ways of personally greeting visitors.

Behind the publication of this book is a dedicated group of docents who went beyond the basic definition of what it means to be a member of this program. In addition to their continuing training, they added classes in advanced sign language and museum interpretation for the deaf. This group, now known as the Docents for the Deaf, pioneered the first such museum program in the western United States. Through the use of simultaneous sign and speech they present the permanent collection and the important temporary exhibitions to the deaf and hearing alike. The tours given by them have been an inspiration and catalyst to other museums interested in starting similar programs. These docents have become one of our most important resources in our attempts to design non-traditional forms for making the art in our galleries more accessible.

Mildred Albronda is one of these wonderful people. She has worked as a Docent for the Deaf since the program began in 1969. Her interests in the hearing disabled linked with her concern for art made Douglas Tilden a natural topic of fascination for her. Mildred's desire to bring art to all people reflects Tilden's earlier efforts to make art a part of everyday life. She has performed an enormous task of collecting the information compiled in this book and has thereby preserved Tilden's contribution.

Douglas Tilden's city sculpture still stands in the San Francisco Bay Area as a monument to his search for beauty and the higher ideals. He recognized the importance of integrating parklands and public places and transforming these to spaces of beauty. Were it not for the great earthquake and fire of 1906, San Francisco would itself be a memorial to Tilden's advanced ideas of city beautification. His sculpture, erected as public monuments in the city he wished to transform into another Athens, remained standing while the buildings crumbled around them.

Tilden was an intriguing man. Although he was deaf in a world not yet ready to understand deafness, his main concerns were with humanity. He looked for a way to bring dignity and beauty into the lives of those around him. How can we not nod in agreement with a man who believed that "Society cannot exist in its fullest vigor unless the importance of art as a constructive force in human progress continues to be recognized. Art makes a state wealthy by showing that life in it is worth while. Art enriches life itself."

Renée Beller Dreyfus
Curator for Education and Interpretation

ACKNOWLEDGEMENTS

This book began when Jane Norman Wilk, deaf actress, drama teacher, and newscaster, first brought Douglas Tilden to my awareness. In September 1972, Jane became the sign-language and museum-interpretation instructor for our Docents for the Deaf program of the Asian Art Museum, and of the Fine Arts Museums of San Francisco: M. H. deYoung Memorial Museum, and the California Palace of the Legion of Honor. Jane gently prodded me into research about the fascinating artistic genius of Douglas Tilden. At first, my findings and photographs resulted in several slide-lectures; later, my many deaf friends who attended these lectures urged me to write something permanent as an inspiration for young deaf people. It is timely now. "Deaf Heritage" is the theme for the Centennial Celebration of the National Association of the Deaf Convention to be held in 1980.

A very personal thanks goes to my son, Eric Albronda, who was the first to actually suggest that I organize my research material into writing a book, and to Dorothy Aggeler, Winifred Cress, and Ann Liska without whose encouragement and assistance in reading and correcting the manuscript in the beginning stages, I would never have continued. Gladys Tilden, the sculptor's daughter, graciously offered information which facilitated enormously my finding reference material about the Tilden family. Preston L. Wright contributed many hours checking lists and copy material in the final stage.

I am deeply indebted to Hugo Schunhoff, former Superintendent of the California School for the Deaf, Berkeley, for his interest in allowing me to pour over old records and boxes in basements and closets at the school to ferret out much of my original material. When Dr. Henry Klopping became Superintendent of the School in 1975, he continued to give his enthusiastic support. Elsa Kleinman, Librarian at the school, cheerfully assisted me in finding old school records and in offering a much needed cup of coffee on a regular basis. Ralph Neesam, Editor of the *California*

News, the school's monthly publication, and newly appointed Director of Outreach and Training, offered continuing valuable suggestions and encouragement throughout the entire project. A tremendous posthumous thanks to Theophilus Hope d'Estrella, Tilden's lifelong friend, who for forty-four years wrote "The Itemizer" column for the *California News* in which he chronicled activities of students and alumni of the school from 1885–1929 providing an accurate and illuminating source of information. Likewise, Caroline Hyman Burnes and Catherine Marshall Ramger have left us an important document in their: *History of the California School for the Deaf, Berkeley, 1860–1960.*

Corrine Hilton, Archives, Gallaudet College, Washington, D.C. has been most thoughtful in supplying me with photocopies of material she has uncovered about Douglas Tilden from the vast resources of the only liberal arts college for the deaf in the world.

For the enormous technical assistance in writing and editing the manuscript, a very special thanks to Max Knight, former principal Editor for the University of California Press, Berkeley. Without his guidance this book never would have come to fruition.

Peter Palmquist, photographer and author, offered advise and assistance in selecting and copying old photographs. His perceptive images of Tilden's statuary in the modern day settings clearly indicates the professional sensitivity of his skills.

I shall be eternally grateful to Eddie Jauregui who insisted that I be reintroduced to T. J. O'Rourke shortly after he established T. J. Publishers, Inc. And finally, the most thanks of all to Mr. O'Rourke who has the vision and interest to produce books contributing to the knowledge of deaf heritage—especially about deaf artists from California.

In addition, I wish to express my gratitude and appreciation to all of the many kind people and institutions who assisted me in obtaining information—particularly to those listed below whose information opened new doors of awareness about the life and times of Douglas Tilden.

Art Institute of Chicago

Bernard Bragg, former Director of the National Theatre of the Deaf

James L. Brown, Park Manager, U.S. Department of Interior, National Park Service, Sagamore Hill National Historic Site, Oyster Bay, New York

Byron Benton Burnes, former President of the National Association of the Deaf

Henry Buzzard, Librarian, New York School for the Deaf, White Plains, New York

California Historical Society staff, San Francisco, California

California School for the Deaf, Berkeley

Raymond Clary, Historian, The John McLaren Society, San Francisco

Commonwealth Club staff, San Francisco

Susan Craig, Art History and Classics Librarian, University of California, Berkeley

E. B. Crocker Art Gallery, Sacramento, California

D.E.A.F. Media, Inc., Oakland, California

Margot Patterson Doss, San Francisco Chronicle, San Francisco

Fillmore Eisenmayer, Architectural Historian, Berkeley

Brother Maurice Flynn, Archivist, Saint Mary's College, Moraga, California

Phil V. Gilbert, Historiographer, Bohemian Club, San Francisco

Katherine Grant, Art and Music Department, Los Angeles Public Library, Los Angeles

Gladys Hanson, Archivist, Archives, San Francisco

Thomas Carr Howe, San Francisco

Leo Jacobs, Oakland

Harry Jacobs, Oakland

John Joyce, President, Joyce Motion Picture Co., Northridge, California

J. R. K. Kantor, University Archivist, Bancroft Library, University of California, Berkeley

Paul Karlstrom, Archives of American Art, Smithsonian Institution, San Francisco

Russ Kingman, Jack London Bookstore, Glen Ellen, California

Margaret Koch, Santa Cruz Sentinel, Santa Cruz, California

Emil Ladner, Berkeley

Waverly Lowell, Archivist, California School for the Deaf, Berkeley

Joyce Lynch, Newscaster, Newsign 4, KRON, San Francisco

Mechanics' Institute Library staff, San Francisco

Harry Mulford, Archivist, San Francisco Art Institute, San Francisco

Alice G. Melrose, Director, National Academy of Design, New York

George Neubert, Curator of Painting and Sculpture, The Oakland Museum, Oakland

Donald Parodi, Historical Society, and Alumni of the California School
  for the Deaf, Berkeley
Oakland Public Library, Oakland
The Oakland Museum Library, Oakland
Olympic Club, San Francisco
Louis Pellandini, Native Sons of the Golden West, San Francisco
Registrar, Historical Art, The White House, Washington, D.C.
Robert Reese, Department of Parks and Recreation, Monterey, California
Santa Cruz Public Library, Santa Cruz, California
San Francisco Public Library—Newspaper Room, San Francisco
Gabriel Sheridan, San Francisco
Albert Shumate, M.D., California Historical Society, San Francisco
Sierra Club, San Francisco
Nikki Silva, Santa Cruz City Museum, Santa Cruz
Maggie Simmons, Paris, France
Jess Smith, Editor, *Deaf American,* Indianapolis, Indiana
Bill Treese, Art Librarian, University of California, Santa Barbara,
  California
University of California Library—Newspaper Room, Berkeley
University of California Library, Santa Cruz
University of Santa Clara, deSaisset Art Gallery, Santa Clara
Tim Wada, Gallaudet College, Washington, D.C.

INTRODUCTION

This book is not meant to be a definitive biography. It is rather a portrait, of one man, a deaf man, Douglas Tilden, and his remarkable accomplishments in the field of art at a time when few artists in the United States possessed the talent and necessary skills to create monumental bronze sculpture.

Today, there is a new sense of growing interest, visual delight, and pride in the discovery of our heritage, manifest in what is now commonly referred to as the American Renaissance in art. Following the Centennial Celebration in Philadelphia in 1876, Americans discovered a new sense of their national past. An era of unprecedented growth began in commerce, industry, finance, and the arts, which marked a turning point in the nation's history. Seventeen years later, in what was called, "the greatest gathering of artists since the Italian Renaissance," the World's Columbian Exposition in Chicago saw the culmination of the European Beaux Arts tradition displayed in architectural and artistic splendor heralding the beginning of a movement to beautify the cities all over the United States. The theme of the Exposition, "Expansion of the American West," marked the time when it was finally decided that the West could be considered part of the civilized America. California heard the call, but San Franciscans wanted *their* art to express *their* enormous pride in *their* own heritage and *their* confidence in *their* destiny. Wresting a nation from the wilderness had consumed most of the energies of the young country of the Pacific slopes. This was the era when monumental sculpture seemed to best demonstrate the apotheosis of the archetypical rugged Western pioneers. Tilden, a native-born Californian, returning to San Francisco in 1894, after six years of study of sculpture in classical Paris, wrote, "I simply felt it in the air—the awakening of San Francisco—the period of intensest art activity in California." Immediately he became involved in a City Beautification Movement.

Previously, during his stay in Paris, Tilden wrote an article, "Art, and What San Francisco Should Do About Her," in which he advocated the building of a publicly supported art museum, the first in San Francisco, in Golden Gate Park, to be copied from the architecture of the Luxembourg Palace in Paris. *The Overland Monthly,* a periodical "devoted to the development of the country," published Tilden's article in May, 1892.

What motivated Tilden's sometimes unique choice of subject? His youthful energy, and his primacy of feeling and love of the great California outdoors, drove him to reach out for understanding and communication through his natural emotional outlet of sculpture. Well schooled in classical art and study, the art of the past provided for Tilden sources of inspiration for the development of a national patriotic art with a "truly American spirit." Tilden's sculptures are documents of his creative impulses reflecting the material American culture, especially of the far Western region of the United States. His first internationally recognized works were of life-size realistic figures from American sports; baseball, boxing, wrestling, and football, all popular pastimes. Tilden felt that he had reached "a point of contact" with the American people because he was "attuned to the passionate liking of youth for athletics."

His Indian and bear theme in the *Bear Hunt,* or man versus nature, caught the romantic imagination of many artists and became America's most original and unique form of sculpture. In this work, where Tilden has shown the Indian and the bear in mortal confrontation, he reflected, "Who wins, will forever be the question—the Indian or the bear?" No grizzly bear has been seen in California since 1924. However, the bronze group remains forever fresh and meaningful, attracting attention by its pure visual image reflecting the French inspired texture with the play of light vibrating over the surfaces.

San Francisco's Mayor, Honorable James Duval Phelan, had long held the belief that "the great conquering power of the world is art." Recognizing Tilden's talents, he appointed him, in 1898, to a city beautification committee and commissioned him to commemorate California heroes and history in monumental bronze statuary. Truth, loyalty, honor, virtue, and noble purpose, all Renaissance ideals, were to be visually symbolized in enduring bronze for all eternity. The citizenry considered Phelan and Tilden true Renaissance men—indeed, Representative Men of California—who dreamed of creating another Athens in San Francisco.

The dynamism of movement and the unorthodox symbols of labor made the *Mechanics* monument the most "lawless composition" in America at the beginning of the twentieth century. Loredo Taft, art historian, wrote, "Not only could no one but Mr. Tilden have made the Mechanics' Fountain, but it could have been done in no other city than San Francisco."

The *California Volunteers,* with its pawing winged horse and fierce Goddess of War posed above the fallen war hero, was acclaimed the most dynamic equestrian war monument in the United States. Tilden's sensitivity in rendering facial expressions is clearly evident in the horse, rider, and heroes. After months of thinking that "war is all horror," he felt that he had achieved his ideal in the idea that "the body dies but the spirit goes on."

Details of the *Admission Day* monument commemorating California's admission to the United States, September 9, 1850, exuberantly portray the spirit of the young western pioneer. Stylistically, Tilden's young miner reflects a highly original naturalism growing out of the cultural forces in California. However, Willis Polk's architectural design for the pedestal and base reflect the iconography of the classic decorative tradition borrowed from Europe. At the top of the pedestal stands Tilden's allegorical bronze figure of a young beautiful female angel holding aloft a book "as yet unwrit upon." She represents California's statehood and personifies the higher virtues of American womanhood.

The quiet ennobling spirit of *Father Junipero Serra,* as portrayed by Tilden, offers a tribute to California's beginnings and to the founding of San Francisco. It is also a monument to Serra's visionary concept of a totally new and different architectural style for California. Theophilus Hope d'Estrella wrote, "Serra founded an architectural style of beauty and simplicity in the great white walls and ample cloisters of the California Missions which is to be perpetuated as a characteristic of California—a nobleness that preaches sermons from the walls."

The City Beautification Movement continues. In 1973, the *Mechanics* was moved a few feet to become the focal point of the much-used new Mechanics Park, a triangle of benches, trees, and pigeons. Mayor Joseph Alioto mastered the dedication ceremony on June 12; no mention was made of Douglas Tilden or his artistry. Four years later, the *Admission Day* statue was returned to Market Street in January 1977, as part of the latest ($24.5 million) beautification program: The Market Street Redevelopment Project. As the noonday sparkling sunshine of April 27, filtered down between the nearby skyscrapers to the festooned platform below, the late Mayor George Moscone rededicated the *Admission Day* monument with a special tribute to the genius of Douglas Tilden. He cited, with pride, Tilden's achievements in spite of his disability. The Mayor then read the Proclamation of Deaf Awareness Week, stepped down from the platform, and handed the document to Leo Jacobs, Chairman of that event. Nicki Norton, standing beside the Mayor, interpreted the entire proceedings in American Sign Language (ASL) to the proud deaf persons, young and old, in the midst of the large noontime crowd. Joyce Lynch, deaf newscaster, KRON TV—NEWSIGN 4, recorded the joyful occasion on camera for her early morning newscast for the deaf in their own language. Tilden would have been pleased. Tilden had always hoped to see his symbol of California statehood placed in front of the Ferry building at the foot of Market Street. Perhaps, eventually in a future wave of beautification, it will be done—it should be.

An exhibition of photographs of Tilden's sculpture, titled: "City Sculpture of Douglas Tilden, 1891–1908," has been planned to open in the late spring of 1980 at the M. H. deYoung Memorial Museum, Golden Gate Park, San Francisco. The Tilden display is planned to make the large travelling exhibition, "American Renaissance, 1876–1917," May 31–August 10, 1980, more relevant to the greater San Francisco Bay Area. Renée Beller Dreyfus, Curator for Education and Interpretation, at the Fine Arts Museums of San Francisco which includes the de Young Museum has an unusually keen sensitivity for greater accessibility to the arts—especially for all the disabled. She has planned the "City Sculpture of Douglas Tilden, 1891–1908" exhibit to coincide with the celebration of Deaf Awareness Month, 1980, in the Bay Area.

Tilden's total output was small. Each monument took months, sometimes years to complete. The support of a generous patron was a necessity. Tilden lived in a time of great change in the arts; he became an old master and did not choose to join the new ranks of artists who wanted to achieve a more personal expression. The change was hastened in San Francisco with the widespread destruction of the earthquake and fire. But out of the ashes, like the Phoenix, arose several of Tilden's monuments unharmed—symbolizing, "it is the fate of art to be immortal."

Mildred Albronda, January 12, 1980.

MONUMENTAL SCULPTURE OF DOUGLAS TILDEN

Dedicated or Unveiled

July 8, 1891 —The *Baseball Player* at the Golden Gate Park, San Francisco. Situated on John F. Kennedy Drive, near tennis courts.

February 28, 1895 —The *Bear Hunt* arrived at the California School for the Deaf, Berkeley. Situated at inner courtyard.

September 5, 1897 —*Admission Day* at Market, Mason, and Turk streets, San Francisco. Now situated at Market, Post, and Montgomery streets.

May 12, 1900 —The *Football Players* at the University of California, Berkeley, near the south-west corner of Life-Science Building.

May 15, 1901 —*Mechanics* at Market, Battery, and Bush streets, San Francisco.

May 30, 1906 —*Oregon Volunteers* at Plaza Park, Portland, Oregon.

August 12, 1906 —*California Volunteers* at Market and Van Ness Avenue, San Francisco. Now situated at Market and Dolores streets.

November 17, 1907 —*Junipero Serra* at Academy of Science and Court Drive, Golden Gate Park, San Francisco.

December 11, 1908 —*Stephen M. White Memorial* in front of the County Courthouse, Los Angeles, California. Now situated in front of the Los Angeles County Law Library, First and Hill streets, Los Angeles.

Circa late 1890s —*Grief,* Valentine Memorial at Cypress Lawn Cemetery, Colma, California.

DOUGLAS TILDEN: PORTRAIT

OF

A DEAF SCULPTOR

CHAPTER I

COMING OF AGE IN BERKELEY

The Origins and the Awakening

1860–1887

Douglas Tilden was the first California-born sculptor to receive recognition outside of the United States. Paris acclaimed his unordinary American-inspired subjects of a *Baseball Player, Tired Boxer, Bear Hunt,* and *Football Players*, all monumental bronze outdoor statuary, three of them now situated in the San Francisco Bay Area. The *Mechanics* monument on Market street, San Francisco, has long been considered his masterpiece; seen by thousands daily, hardly noticed by some, treasured by many. The figures of *Junipero Serra, Admission Day,* and *California Volunteers* are reminders of glorious moments in San Francisco's past. Tilden became affectionately known as the father of sculpture in California. This distinction he achieved in the face of enormous odds; he could neither hear nor speak. His is a story of persistent courage and stubborn faith in his own abilities, of extraordinary success; and in the end, of isolation, torment, and a brave fight to overcome the onslaught of forces beyond his control.

Origins

Tilden was born May 1, 1860, at Chico, California, to William Peregrine Tilden and Catherine Hecox Tilden, both pioneers to the land of the Pacific slopes. Tilden's father and paternal grandfather were physicians in Maryland. Their ancestor, Marmaduke Tylden, came from Great Tyldens, near Marden Kent, England in 1658, settling at Great Oaks Manor, Kent County, Maryland, on an estate which at one time is said to have comprised thirty-six thousand acres[1]. Dr. Tilden, Douglas's father, after finishing his residency in Baltimore hospitals, moved to Pennsylvania where he was a Fellow of the College of Physicians of Philadelphia before journeying to California in 1855 or 1856, where he met and married the talented young Catherine Hecox still in her teens. They settled on the beautiful Rancho Chico, belonging to the early trail blazer John Bidwell, where Douglas was born. Dr. Tilden, a Union Democrat, was elected to the State Assembly, where in turn he was elected Resident Physician of the Stockton Insane Asylum. The family moved to Stockton in 1861. Four years later, during a scarlet-fever epidemic, Douglas, then age five, lost his hearing. What was more unusual, after the prolonged bout of fever he also lost his ability to use his voice. He remained deaf and without speech throughout his life.

Tilden's mother's family were even earlier pioneers in California. On March 23, 1846, little Catherine Hecox celebrated her fifth birthday clutching her new homemade doll and getting into a covered wagon with her parents, her two sisters, Sarah and Ellen, and her baby brother, Adna H. Hecox, at Apple River, Illinois, starting a trek west that would end seven months later in the Santa Clara valley, California. Catherine's father, Adna A. Hecox, a cabinet maker and part-time Methodist Episcopal minister, her mother, Margaret Hamer Hecox, and the children were members of a party of fifty-seven persons led by Joseph Aram. Four other parties joined them as the wagon train moved west; one of them was led by George Donner.[2]

From an account his maternal grandfather gave him, Douglas related in a newspaper article many years later: "Three of the five parties separated from the main body . . . beyond Laramie, to go to Oregon. . . . After the three Oregon-bound parties went on their trail, the Donner and Aram parties parted company. The Aram party chose to follow the old Bidwell trail of 1844 up to the southern extremity of Montana and then follow the Bear River down to Thousand Wells. . . . The Aram party dashed across the Humboldt basin in company of the Indian Chief Truckee. On October 1st they sighted the Sacramento Valley from the summit of the Sierras."[3] The Donner party took off to the southwest and was later trapped in the Sierra Nevada with the well-known tragic results.

After a brief rest near Sutter's Fort, the Hecoxes moved on to the Santa Clara valley. There the immigrants were exposed to "great suffering from lack of food and from illness."[4] In December 1846, shortly before or after

Christmas, Hecox, weakened by typhoid fever, preached a sermon "Remember how short time is" for the funeral service of a young woman who had succumbed to the dread disease. "This was, without a doubt the first Protestant sermon ever preached within the present limits of the State of California."[5]

The Hecox family remained in Santa Clara for the winter, 1846–1847 "occupying one of the old dilapidated Mission buildings and taking an active part in the war with the Mexicans." Mrs. Hecox told her daughter Catherine later: "In spite of all the hardships . . . in that dark, miserable hole where we were confined, with hunger and sickness within and enemies without, we started a little school and our children commenced their education." The dangers and hardships of that winter made Hecox eager to leave in the spring for the safer and peaceful Santa Cruz nearby on February 20, 1847, by ox-team.[6]

Eight days later, little Catherine and her family settled in a cabin on the Soquel River, near Santa Cruz, where her father worked rebuilding a washed-out saw mill. Finding "drunkenness was exceedingly prevalent," Hecox signed up several "topers" for the first temperance movement in California. On May 1, 1847, he preached the first Protestant sermon in Santa Cruz for a young man killed by a falling tree.[7] Hecox felt a strong attachment to Santa Cruz and decided to make it the permanent home for his family; he was eager to work for the improvement and growth of the community.

In 1848 Hecox was seized by the gold fever and joined a party of men who found the rich diggings of Hangtown. Four months later, he returned to Santa Cruz with "gold enough for every comfort that money could buy: but that was not much in those days."[8] Santa Cruz made him its last alcalde. During the Civil War days, he became justice of the peace and county treasurer. After the war, in 1869, he was appointed custodian of the new United States lighthouse, a post which he held until his death in 1883.[9]

Early Boyhood

During Douglas's boyhood, the warm, loving, nurturing environment of his grandparents' home at the lighthouse was a haven for him and some young deaf friends on weekends and on vacations. Many of Douglas's early childhood impressions of textures, forms, and shapes came from visits to the lighthouse and from tramping around and over the rocks on the nearby beach. From his grandfather's skilled hands he learned carpentry and cabinet making. Mrs. Hecox's friendliness encouraged many to call her grandma. She often recounted stories of the overland journey in the covered wagon. With some shyness, she recalled: "I'm ashamed to say I was not one of those brave spirited women who rise above all trials, and sit smiling in the air. I was afraid of everything and hated the discomforts of the way we travelled."[10] She bore her lot for ninety-three years, becoming a strong supportive factor in Tilden's development.

Douglas tramped along beside his grandfather on jaunts around the countryside and to the seashore. Shortly after Adna A. Hecox settled in Santa Cruz, he began collecting shells and also Indian relics and artifacts from inland. These were kept in the lighthouse on public display. Douglas often helped collect shells and identify them. His young aunt, Laura, born after the family arrived in Santa Cruz, also became an eager collector. After grandfather Hecox's death in 1883, this daughter, Laura, kept the light until it was put under automatic control in 1904. The Santa Cruz City Museum was started at this time when Laura Hecox and her mother gave their collections to the city of Santa Cruz with a gift deed.[11]

California School for the Deaf

Early in their marriage, William and Catherine Tilden came face to face with the seemingly unsurmountable task of educating their young son Douglas after he lost his faculties to hear or speak. It so happened that on March 17, 1860, a group of twenty-three ladies met at the Oriental Hotel, Market and Bush streets, and organized a "Society for the Instruction and Maintenance of the Indigent Deaf and Dumb, and the Blind." A few weeks later, May 1, 1860—the day Douglas was born—the first school for deaf children in California opened its doors on Tehama Street in San Francisco in a rented cottage.[12] At age five years and nine months, January 25, 1866, Douglas Tilden enrolled in the California School for the Deaf as it is now called. A friend said that the only conspicuous thing about him was his red scarf, from which he got his name sign.[13] Deaf children create a gesture signifying some characteristic near the face or body as a way of referring to a person's name in the sign language of the deaf—in this instance, a touch of the index finger to the lips, for red, followed by a downward sweeping stroke of the middle finger, for scarf, to the base of the neck, meaning "red scarf." Shortly after Douglas' admission to the school, Dr. Tilden was reelected to the State Assembly, and as a member of the Legislative Education Committee helped to select a new site in the Berkeley hills for the school, where it still stands. The move was completed in 1869 and it was noted that "coyotes, foxes, wild cats, and rattlesnakes haunted this neighborhood." Dr. Tilden returned to private practice in Chico, where he died in May 1873.

Douglas became the first pupil under Dr. Warring Wilkinson as principal. "The first boy who entered the institution after I took charge of it," Dr. Wilkinson recorded, "was a bright little fellow about six years old, and of most excellent parentage." Wilkinson continued with his story:

> One day, not many weeks afterwards, without provocation, he knocked off another boy's cap. I happened to come along just then, and I told him to pick up the cap and give it back. He refused. Telling the aggrieved lad to leave his cap on the ground, I led the aggressor to my room and, taking him on my knee, I tried to make him understand how naughty he had been, when suddenly he struck me in the face with a long tin pill-box which he held in his hand. I took him by both arms and gave him one severe shake. . . . 'Now will you pick up the cap?' 'Yes.' He went out with me, and handed the boy his cap. They embraced each other, and I went about my work. I have no recollection of ever having had occasion to discipline him afterwards. The boy is now a distinguished sculptor, many of whose works adorn the city of San Francisco.[14]

Dr. Wilkinson had a wide range of interests with emphasis on the arts. When the school moved in 1869, it became the first state institution in Berkeley. Four years later, 1873, Dr. Wilkinson entered a close relationship with the new Universtiy of California when it first opened its doors on the Berkeley campus. Several deaf students were successfully graduated there, athletic contests were held together, and both schools shared an interest in developing the hamlet of Berkeley. Douglas thrived in the aesthetic atmosphere created by Dr. Wilkinson's enthusiasm for California, which the teacher expressed in the West's outstanding literary magazine, *The Overland Monthly;* "California secures favorable conditions for physical development and intellectual activity. . . . There is little reverence for anything but success. . . . California has no traditions, she has something better; the promise of a glorious future. . . . Every work of

Art, . . . is determined by a variety of social and intellectual influences . . . to get at the life motive of any epoch we need to get at its Art as well as its Literature."[15] Dr. Wilkinson saw to it that art education was an integral part of the curriculum of his deaf pupils.

Douglas was an alert student who made rapid progress in his studies. Dr. Wilkinson describes him as "a bright attractive little fellow of more than average intelligence, of somewhat violent temper, but not difficult to control."[16] After he had been in the school only two months, he went with Dr. Wilkinson to Sacramento to help with an exhibition of the students before the Legislature. On another occasion, they went by boat up the Sacramento River. En route, Douglas had difficulty eating his supper because he was absorbed in watching the forceful-looking gentleman with his trimmed beard seated at the head of the table—Governor Leland Stanford, a colossus of his time, and a friend of his father.[17]

"San Francisco was not like Athens, a city of ten thousand statues," recalled Tilden many years later. "No, there was only one lone figure in some hard substance, made by a wandering Italian sculptor and erected on Sixth Street, soon after the assassination of Lincoln; it represented the emancipator holding aloft the letter which was to free millions of human beings."[18] This statue must have made a deep imprint on Douglas' young mind as he roamed around the intriguing streets and waterfront of San Francisco near his school and home. Thirty years later he remembered: "I could not pass it without stopping, completely fascinated by its lifelikeness and dramatic gesture, and the memory of those days even now inclines me toward a compassionate judgment of its faults and a certain fondness for it that a Californian must feel for every thing connected with the large, glorious and turbulent days of the Golden Era."[19]

Douglas seemed to be always interested in art. As a small child he modeled figures with mud, carved wood with his penknife, and painted pictures whenever the opportunity arose. In later life, he laughed when he remembered one creative attempt to picture making: "The nearest example in which I emulated the example of Benjamin West who made a brush out of his cat's hair was: When I was nine or ten years old, I stole some bluewash and after pounding it into powder and properly mixing it with water, I began to think how I could find a brush. It occurred to me that my own hair would do; so I nipped off a tuft and fastened it to the end of a stick."[20] During his school years in Berkeley, Douglas frequently joined drawing classes and enthusiastically attended wood-carving sessions.

The honing of his aesthetic perceptions was furthered when Douglas joined the Excelsior Debating Society at the California School for the Deaf in his early teens. He remained an active member for several years. The "debating" took the form of fingers flying spelling out words from the manual alphabet and expressive gestures gracefully creating visual patterns of thought. The sign language of the deaf is a gesture system of symbols for thought and emotion. It is the "listening eye" to those for whom it is a necessary form of communication. Douglas eagerly joined in the detailed, well-planned debates about Art versus Nature which continued for several months. He was obliged to accept the role of secretary of the society—a chore he disliked. After a short time he announced that he was resigning but his resignation was not accepted. According to the minutes, "Tilden became enraged at this, refused to write the minutes, and said he would run away." Now the members voted to expell him.[21] This episode provides a hint of his developing character. His stubborness and his impatience with his fellows created difficulties for Tilden throughout much of his life.

Teacher Career

An honor student, Douglas graduated from the California School for the Deaf in June 1879 and successfully passed the exams for entrance into the nearby University of California. He registered as a student for the fall of 1879. However, Dr. Wilkinson wrote later:

> During vacation I received a letter from Mrs. Tilden saying that Douglas was very unhappy; that he did not want to go to the University but feared to tell me because he thought I would be disappointed, and that his ideal life was that of a mechanic. I wrote for him to come see me. He did so, and showed me some drawings which indicated considerable inventive faculty. I then went to work to obtain for him a position in a machine shop. I could not obtain work for him because of his deafness, the family was in straitened circumstances, I suggested about mid October that he come teach till an opening in mechanical pursuits opened.[22]

Douglas accepted the teaching position and stayed on for eight years. He worked diligently at teaching, keeping notes about his own methods of instruction. He began to write articles about educating the young deaf, which were published in various journals of the deaf in the United States. *The Overland Monthly* published his essay "Deaf Mutes and their Education" in 1885.[23] Tilden thought he had received what the young teachers considered the blue ribbon of distinction, in 1887, when three of his essays—"A Forgotten Page of an Institution History,"[24] "Articulation in a New Light,"[25] and "Signs and Words"[26]—were all accepted in the prestigious *American Annals of the Deaf* for that year. Following these essays, he tried his hand at fiction: *The Overland Monthly* published his perceptive story of the trials and tribulations of a young deaf artist, "The Artist's Testament," which Tilden wrote under the name of Clarence Stairly.[27]

Great Outdoors

Tilden loved the great outdoors. Tramping through the hills of Berkeley, hiking and camping in the Russian River area and the high Sierra mountains, influenced his later concern for Western subjects in his sculpture. In July 1881, Tilden journeyed with friends by river boat to Stockton from there on horseback to Yosemite. Yosemite, by then, had become a symbol for all of California. Tilden would undoubtedly have agreed with Kevin Starr, eminent historian and writer, who wrote after Tilden's time: "You get a sense of power from these wide views. . . . Topographically spacious, California allowed for an expansion of personality as the self grew outward to fill the large vistas which the eyes always possessed."[28] Tilden has left us in writing a glimpse of his youthful exuberance: "We descended into the Valley . . . on the trail below Cloud's Rest, we found a rope hanging down the face of a smooth cliff one thousand feet high. I determined to climb that rope hand over hand." He tied his horse to a bush, seized the hanging rope and began the climb up the rounding surface of the Dome, leaning back as the climb necessitated, testing each length of·rope between the pins by a few jerks before pulling his whole weight on it. "I reached the top of the mound which proved to be the crest of the famous Half Dome, an acre or so of solid granite. Crawling flat on my breast, I reached the edge of the other side of the dome and looked straight down one mile into the Valley."[29] Dr. William A. Caldwell, his companion of that morning, related later: "Since that day, Mr. Tilden has climbed to the dizzy heights of fame and has won an honorable and permanent place among the artists of the world.

It is not unlikely that he has been influenced to some extent in his choice of subjects by the wild free life of the mountains, a taste of which he enjoyed during that summer in the Sierras."[30] Tilden's sculpture expresses the growth of an expansive feeling for all things Californian—the essence of his art.

In the summer of 1882, accompanied by Theophilus d'Estrella, his life-long deaf friend, he camped out at Big Tree Camp near Russian River for three weeks, to sketch "there amidst the beauties of Nature—under her inspiration and guidance."[31]

Awakening to Sculpture

In 1882 Tilden spent one month during summer vacation at the San Francisco School of Design studying drawing and painting under the guidance of Virgil Williams, director of the school.

However, in the summer of 1883, he discovered the joys of sculpture. "That was the summer that influenced the rest of my life." On a visit home, he saw a brother modeling some clay and was fascinated. He wondered whether he could do the same. "A lurking consciousness that I would be famous some day, a flitting feeling that I should and could do something that fame would proclaim to the world with the blast of a trumpet had always haunted me. Was it to be through writing? painting? inventing? I knew nothing about sculpture."[32] He hastened to the studio of his brother's teacher, Marion Wells, and then left for us in writing a glimpse of his wonder: "I had never been in such a workshop, what a world of new sensation was then unfolded to me. It was like breaking into a treasure house. The atmosphere seemed to suffocate and intoxicate me. . . . There were plaster casts of former modelings of masterpieces and of dead men, faces, busts, masses of white stone in the process of cutting, the Turkish curtain stretched over the sofa in the corner with the inevitable pipe and bowl of tobacco by its side; the air smelt of dampness, the unswept floor, the marble dust, the delightful confusion everywhere!"[33]

The sculptor Wells accepted Douglas Tilden as a pupil for one month. At the end of that time, he said, "I can not teach you any more." Tilden felt that he had "learned the hang of it. But is sculpture execution alone? No, it is much more than that, and it can never be learned from a book of rules alone or merely mastered by practice and that and many more things I learned in after years."[34]

Tilden purchased a barrel of clay, moved into a deserted laundry shed on the campus, and set up what may have been the first sculpture studio in Berkeley. He returned to teaching in the fall, and in his leisure continued modeling four years longer. Tilden dreamed of and longed for study in Paris—the mecca of most would-be sculptors. He was satisfied that he had "fallen upon" the right vocation but "doubts assailed me at every step." His modeling of the *Tired Wrestler*—a young athletic male nude figure, head bowed—so interested the Board of Trustees of the California School for the Deaf that they gave him a first loan of five hundred dollars for study in New York.[35]

In June 1887, he resigned from his teaching post. That summer he spent mostly with his family at the lighthouse in Santa Cruz reading, sketching, and wandering along the seashore. September finally arrived and Tilden eagerly wrote: "It was therefore with fear and trembling and a high resolve to do my best, that I . . . left California."[36]

CHAPTER II

FAREWELL, BERKELEY

Letters from New York and Paris

1887–1894

On September 11, 1887, the day before his departure for New York, Tilden sent his friend Theophilus d'Estrella a farewell note. It was a poignant poetic outpouring of Tilden's deep love and tender affection for all he was leaving behind in Berkeley: "Tomorrow I leave thee Berkeley. Ambition calls: I have been dreaming of realms fair to conquer and am eager to be gone. Sometimes me thinks it is all a mistake to leave thee, Berkeley, but if ever I come back a wanderer, I know but one place besides home where I may find a haven for a weary spirit; it is thee, my rose-embowered Berkeley. Farewell, Berkeley, farewell!"[1]

On the next day, Monday, September 12, Tilden left California for New York, where he was to spend the next eight months studying the sculptor's art. A short article in the school newsweekly wished him farewell and expressed the hope that he may "win credit to himself and add one more to the long list of artists who have shown to the world that deafness is not an absolute bar to success."[2]

Letters from New York

Tilden's letters to d'Estrella, written between September and December 1887, describe his experiences and reactions during those months.

I came over the continent in six days. I never thought as much of California as I do after that three thousand miles' ride. California is simply a noble State in comparison with others. But I must say the 440

11

miles run through New York opened my eyes to its resources and the absolute prettiness of its scenery. There is no such in California. Verdure even in this season is profuse everywhere. The rural scenes are just those which inspired Washington Irving in his descriptions.

San Francisco beats New York City for pretty ladies, spacious streets, noble stores like Shreve & Co., or the White House, the roominess of the Palace Hotel or the Baldwin, and the Park. . . . The buildings here are much, much finer externally and internally. Studios are as plentiful here as tailoring establishments are in San Francisco. I am now living in one in partnership with a deaf-mute crayon artist.

Ready-made clothes are generally worn here. The California people are as a rule better dressed.[3]

Tilden's curiosity was whetted when he visited the oral "School for the Improved Instruction of the Deaf" on 67th Street. He wanted to know whether the oral teachers actually discarded signs:

I wanted to see what an oral school is, in its off-hours. . . . I was first led into the boys' sitting-room; and imagine my surprise, on every side, signs were being used with the facility of long practice. . . .

I was introduced to the supervisor who could talk as well as I in signs; and the first question I asked him: "How is it that signs are used here contrary to the express declaration of the oralists that it is not done?"

He laughed as if my question was not an uncommon one and said that Prof. Greenberger by no means prohibited the use of signs outside of the schoolrooms. "It is but natural," he added, "that the deaf should be using their own vernacular."[4]

In another letter to d'Estrella, Tilden recounts his thoughts about his academic instruction and his disappointment with his instructors.

I am already at work at the National Academy. The instructors do not give any one more than five minutes of individual attention in a day or even perhaps a week. We are supposed to be advanced enough to shift for ourselves. The students, except in certain respects, are by no means more advanced. I am much disappointed at this state of affairs as I imagined that the students were so advanced that I would gain much by association. I gain but little.

I like New York more and more all the time and wonder if I shall ever want to get back to California.[5]

Fall and winter, 1887, and spring, 1888, in New York City offered the young art student a widening vista of visual experiences. Every morning Tilden attended classes at the National Academy School of Fine Arts; in the evening, he studied at the Gotham Student's League. He quickly advanced from drawing antique casts in charcoal to the drawing of live models. Tilden wanted a firm foundation in drawing and did not work in clay that year. He took fresh inspiration as he walked past Augustus Saint-Gaudens' much talked about memorial monument of the Civil War hero, *Admiral David Glascow Farragut* in Madison Square Park. This monument by the master sculptor in the United States, was to lead the way for Tilden and others with its simplified naturalism and intense nationalistic spirit. A great paralyzing snow storm in the spring gave him a lasting impression of the powers of nature. In April 1888, he wrote to d'Estrella about it:

> I survived the great storm. . . . We had a regular siege of three days—no mail, no milktrains, no meat supply, no telegraph service, no surface or elevated lines running! What a little presumptuous creature man is once he is in the toils of nature. He stutters, is pompous, and talks of chaining lightening, bottling up steam and boxing up fire but by and by a blizzard comes around and he loses his head, howls, pays fifty dollars for a bed or dies in the snow drift—all because only two feet of snow fell![6]

Tilden and a roommate, known only as Bailey, spent long hours at night in their tiny studio room talking about "the far-off almost mythical Paris which, by a mere wave of her wand, seemed to make an artist of anybody."[7] With their limited funds, they decided to travel by steerage, but, after investigation of the ship's hold and not liking the close quarters they saw, they decided on the next cheapest—a second-class accomodation on a Dutch line. On May 10, Tilden wrote to d'Estrella: "By the time you read this, I will be in mid-ocean! I start for Paris via Rotterdam Saturday morning."[8]

Letters from Paris

Fourteen days after Tilden and Bailey sailed from New York, they arrived late one Saturday evening in Paris. The next morning, they hurriedly dressed and went out onto the streets. "Paris burst on us in all her glory, we drinking in the sunshine with our mouths open, our purses almost empty, and not a single friend in sight and our knowledge of the French language next to nil."[9]

Tilden wrote home to the California School for the Deaf for his second-year loan. Then he visited the Salon: "For the first time in my life I became conscious of whatever strength there was in me." As he looked over the "sea of sculpture"—eight hundred separate pieces—"generally with one leg straight and the other leg bent with its foot resting on something," he thought the quality of excellence was unequal, and said to himself: "I could do as well—I *would* be a sculptor. Whatever intentions I might have had as to an academic course in sculpture, I brushed aside (I, however, took lessons in charcoal drawing in evenings as before); I took a studio instead and, taking off my coat, began the *Baseball Player*."[10] This was the statue of a man in baseball attire about to throw a ball. Tilden's enthusiasm for his new life continued. In September he wrote to d'Estrella urging him to visit Paris.

> In Paris! Am I awake or sleeping and dreaming? You can hardly believe it yourself. A thousand times we have talked of going to Paris: Paris was ever our theme and now I am writing—where? Why, in the very city where Louis the Grand held his high carnivals and Napoleon used to ride at the head of his shouting legions!
>
> My advice to you is to come by all means. . . . You will never know what California is like till you have come East and crossed the Atlantic. But Paris is a grand city and worth seeing.
>
> I have seen the Salon—that awful word at which we bow down and worship. Sculpture was not remarkable. The paintings were much better.[11]

The French Way of Life

Shortly after, Tilden wrote d'Estrella his observations on the cost of living, the zestful life of the French, and the working women of Paris.

> You ask about the cost of living here. It is dear till one knows the Parisian way of living. Only the French people and the artists can live cheap. I live this way: For morning, cafe au lait (a bowl of coffee and a roll of bread) which costs 4 sous or cents; for lunch, a roll of bread and

fruits costing 10 sous, and for dinner from 1½ to 2½ francs (30 to 50 cents). . . .

It is amusing to see with what a zest the French go into the enjoyment of mere trifles. The French even dance in the street! There is no such thing about their dancing as the bored air of a social martyr. The partners rush into each other's arms and hug in a way our dancing master would not approve of, and away they whirl.

The French, it seems to me either live to a good old age or die by the enemy's shell. On the anniversary of the taking of the Bastille, I counted on one side of a single block two hundred aged persons demurely sitting in the shade of trees, drinking wine and exchanging reminiscences. They don't drink water in Paris; does wine superinduce longevity?

Women work like men; it shocks a new comer to see that. So muscular and savage-looking are those vegetable women that I should not wonder if tomorrow morning, I see them march by, bearing on the tops of spears the heads of the victims of their fury.[12]

In November 1888, an anniversary banquet was held to honor the memory of Abbé de l'Eppé, who is credited with originating the sign language of the deaf as it is used today. Tilden had learned enough of the French sign language to give a short presentation about the deaf in America:

In harbor of New York, there stands a monument—a legacy of France. It represents Liberty Enlightening the World. . . . But, Monsieur le President, there is yet another monument, also a legacy of France, the splendour of which outshines the Statue of Liberty and reaches out all over the land. It represents the emancipation of the intellectual status of the deaf.

A hundred years ago there was not a single school for the deaf in America. Today there are some fifty institutions. . . . From New York to California the same system of education is being adapted, the same hand alphabet is used, the same sign language is in vogue, all patterned after those invented by the parent school of France . . . . Believe me, Messieurs, the deaf of America hold the memory of the priest in fervent veneration. Allow me as their representative, to salute the bust of Abbé de l'Eppé.[13]

Tilden worked hard that first winter with some guidance from Paul Chopin, a deaf Salon medalist. As the months passed and the clay model of the *Baseball Player* began to take shape, Tilden wrote that he began to realize the vast chasm between conception and execution and how difficult it was to express through any medium, what one sees or feels. "Persons warned me," he said, "that it was no joke to try to get into the Salon, since the city was full of artists, and, out of the thousands of sculptures submitted to the jury, only from 750–1000 could be chosen. . . . This, combined with a chastened spirit, began to give me misgivings."[14]

Paris of 1889 was aswarm with millions of visitors to her International Exposition to commemorate the centenary of the Revolution. The chief feature, the Eiffel Tower, 984 feet, amazed the world. Artists wanted their works to be displayed; the awards or lack of them could make or break an artist. Tilden with high hopes submitted the *Baseball Player* (sometimes called the *National Game*) to the American section of the Exposition which had an American jury, thinking they would be less demanding and more patriotic, and that he would stand a better chance. He had to wait a long time until the jury called at the studio. "Finding I could neither hear nor speak," Tilden recalled later, "it looked curiously from me to the figure and went out with a single remark to the effect that I would get a letter by and by. No tiding, however, came till the last day on which the Salon received the entries for its own separate exhibition. That morning the postman brought a letter which I hastily opened. It read: 'not accepted.' "[15]

The Salon

Tilden undismayed sent for a wagon to transport his statue to the Salon des Artistes Francaises on the Champs Elysees. The plaster cast arrived shortly before the doors closed on the final day of acceptance of entries for judgment. Several days passed until, at last, the anxious Tilden received a letter, marked Ministry of Fine Arts, containing a single word: "Accepté."[16] It was an enormous success for the young, untried sculptor. Even the great Rodin had sought the approbation of the Salon, necessary for opening the doors leading to public commissions, fame, and fortune.

Elated with his acceptance, Tilden indulged in many hours of visiting and studying at the Louvre and other galleries and just tramping around exploring the streets of Paris. He wrote about his observations in *The Weekly News:*

The French are a most sociable people. . . . The city is one vast home in itself. . . . The streets are not the draymen's, but the people's, in which to enjoy life, while it lasts; the boulevards are wide and fine, and shady with trees and at regular intervals are seats; where several avenues meet, there are squares with beds of flowers, statues, and playing fountains; cafes are everywhere with tables and chairs lining the sidewalk, at which you sit, order your ices, gossip, read, play or watch the unceasing streaming in and out of the people. The French love the streets, the trees, and flowers, and the open air, they leave them only to sleep.[17]

On Sundays, Tilden often dined with his friends. One afternoon, he drove into the country with his deaf friend and advisor, Paul Chopin. Seeing the peasants at work in the fields prompted him to write: "Even the women do men's work—those women worn out with childbirth! [Jean Francois] Millet has shown us the dark side of peasantry—its woes, sufferings, and degradations; his pictures are no exaggeration. . . . We can only be thankful that our home is America where reverence for womanhood is the palladium of its greatness."[18]

D'Estrella's Visit

In July 1889 d'Estrella visited Tilden in Paris. We can just imagine the pleasant reunion these two friends enjoyed with their fingers flying. Later, returning to the California School for the Deaf, d'Estrella wrote lengthy articles in the *Weekly News* about his summer trip. He was impressed by Independence Day: "We both celebrated the glorious American Fourth of July by visiting Buffalo Bill's Wild West Show. I was glad, almost to tears, to see the beautiful Union flag, gallantly borne by Buffalo Bill on his black steed. This show was the greatest thing of the day at Paris with the exception of the exposition. As many as 25,000 persons attended a single performance, and the rush was so great that the police was forced to interfere."[19] All over Europe, American Indians, cowboys, and American animals began to appear in paintings and sculpture. Buffalo Bill Cody's antics from the Wild West piqued the creative minds of the artists.

At the First International Congress for the Deaf held in Paris in July 1889 as part of the Exposition, Tilden was elected vice-president. He chaired heated sessions, discussing whether the deaf could be taught best by signs or by the pure oral method. The oral method espoused speech training and lip reading, and rejected the use of all signs. Differences between the two methods of teaching had led to years of controversy about the superiority of one method over the other. Tilden thought the sign language of the deaf was a natural and therefore superior means of expression of thoughts, of feelings, and of concepts for communication between the deaf. He believed in teaching speech to those who could benefit. He deprecated any method which excluded competent deaf-mute teachers from the classroom. After several days of debates the Congress adopted unanimously Tilden's resolution that the American combined system, which used both speech and signs, was the best method for the largest number of deaf persons.

Entertainment at the Congress included a major party at Versailles and a grand banquet at the Hotel Continental. The table was for two hundred persons. Only a few were women because ladies did not think it proper to mix with men in public. After dinner Tilden addressed the group using sign language. There were twenty delegates from the United States; d'Estrella was one from California. Months later, after reading reports of this Congress, Tilden was disturbed by what he considered the lack of organization among the deaf. Almost in anguish, in an article titled "Oignons Sautes," he wrote: "No Congress of the Deaf can be of any use or sense as long as we ourselves are not a factor in society. We have, and can command, no influence socially and politically. We are, in every relation we have with the outside world, entirely passive."[20] He devoted himself from then on to attempting to change this situation.

Honorable Mention

During his second winter in Paris, following the success of the *Baseball Player,* Tilden wanted to create another young athletic male figure. Working for several months to produce the model of a tired boxer, he described his relief, when the statue was finally finished the following spring:

> Tomorrow the moulders will arrive to convert the clay figure [of the *Tired Boxer*] into plaster; they will make a mess of my studio after the manner of all plasterers and a little disarrange my peace with the world, but that will not matter. After that, professional statue movers will arrive with the implements of their trade; they will use rollers,

bars and a wooden frame to hoist the statue on the wagon, and then take it away. The destination is a palace over the Seine river, a ponderous affair built of stone, iron and glass, and called the Palace des Industries where the Salon was held.[21]

On June 4, 1890, the superintendent of the California School for the Deaf received a cablegram with the single word: "Honorable." To receive honorable mention at the Salon was the high water mark for an American sculptor. No American sculptor had won higher recognition; "honorable" was all the most famous sculptor of the day, Augustus Saint-Gaudens, had received for his statue of *Admiral Farragut*. D'Estrella commented in his *Itemizer* column: "It certainly is most creditable that a young deaf-mute, a stranger in a strange land, a youth to fortune and to fame unknown, should have his *first* work admitted and his second work obtain honorable mention."[22]

In October 1890, Tilden wrote to d'Estrella that he would begin the *Death Grip (Bear Hunt)* — a group showing five figures, two Indians and three bears — next year; during the winter and spring he would make studies in the Jardin des Plantes where the animal sculptor Emmanuel Fremiet, considered then to be the foremost animal sculptor in the world, taught. Also, that he was working on the statuette, "The *Young Acrobat*."[23]

Baseball Player Goes to San Francisco

In September, the bronze *Baseball Player* was shipped from Paris to San Francisco where it was first revealed to the public in San Francisco's most important art show until that time. The Art Loan Exhibition of foreign masters was opened in Shreve's art rooms "for sweet charities sake" on February 28, 1891. San Francisco had no public art gallery, hence rare paintings were seen only by the generosity of private citizens sharing their collections. Included in this exhibit were works of Rembrandt, Gainsborough, Constable, Delacroix, Courbet, Monet, and Mrs. William Crocker's *"Man with the Hoe"* by Jean Francois Millet (today still a favorite in San Francisco). The only work by an American artist in the display was Tilden's *Baseball Player,* or *The National Game* as it was originally titled. Prominently displayed, it was the principal attraction and enthusiastically received. W. E. Brown of the Southern Pacific Railroad

Company bought the statue and presented it to the Art Commission for Golden Gate Park. It was "so prized by the art connoisseurs that replicas have been ordered by Tiffany's of New York" announced the evening newspapers.[24] How many replicas and their whereabouts now are unknown.

The unveiling in Golden Gate Park, July 8, 1891, was a simple ceremony; the statue was placed south of the *Garfield Monument* across the Main Drive (now John F. Kennedy Drive), where it still stands. The statue has become a memorial to the sculptor. The inscription reads: "Presented by a Friend of the Sculptor as a Tribute to his Energy, Industry and Ability." One newspaper man noted the likeness of the statue to Tilden.

When Tilden's desire to remain in Paris and to continue his studies was brought to Brown's attention, he gave Tilden a sufficient monthly allowance to remain in Paris several more years. Brown, swept up in his own philanthropic desires to be a patron of the arts, wanted to help develop a California sculptor.

To show his gratitude, Tilden presented his benefactor with the statuette, *Young Acrobat,* a work in marble and bronze with gold plated base, exhibited in the 1892 Salon. When it was later exhibited in the Mark Hopkins Institute of Art, it was described as "an odd and pretty conceit . . . it consists of the muscular arm of a man on the outspread hand of which sits a baby. . . . The timid baby, will, however, attract most attention. The half-fearful expression of the little acrobat, the one foot steadied against the brawny arm, the other drawn up, the half outstretched hands, all portray the evident insecurity, to the baby's mind, of the seat it occupies."[25] The present whereabouts of this treasure is unknown.

Brown also arranged for the subscription purchase of the *Tired Boxer* for the Olympic Club. The list of donors included the "big four"— Stanford, Crocker, Hopkins, and Huntington. Tilden later recounted: "Superb men all moving in the highest walks of life; the subscription book will be an heirloom." The bronze statue was permanently placed in the foyer of the club and displayed for the first time at the dedication ceremonies of the Olympic Club's beautiful new building on Post Street, January 2, 1893.[26]

After completing the model of the *Young Acrobat* and having the security of Brown's patronage, Tilden felt the need for a larger studio. On July 10, 1891, he happily writes d'Estrella of his new address and of his ideas for grander sculpture: "I am now writing in my new studio—No. 14, Rue de Moulin de Buerre, where I am quite comfortably settled. I now have a fine iron bedstead and a famous mattress. I slept on a sofa for the three past years and will have nothing to complain of in my lot[27]. . . . A reporter, writing in the magazine *Argonaut* under the name of "Parisina" gives us a first-hand glimpse into Tilden's studio:

> A favorite haunt of sculptors. No. 14 in that out of way, tortuous street is a conglomeration of wooden tenements, built on either side of a broad alley inclosed by iron gates . . . turning the door handle, I found myself in a large studio, sun and light streaming through the high windows. . . . Tilden was not in his studio. . . . A winding stair leads up from it to an apartment above, and on the door is an invite to pass without knocking. My greeting fell on deaf ears. . . . But we were soon installed with paper and pen and our chat began. I found an intellectual face, speaking eyes, and fair moustache, well knit figure about middle height, with hands long and nervous, the hands of an artist. . . . On a table was a bust of Dante, above hung—over some photographs—a cast of Michelangelo's *Slave*.[28]

The *Argonaut* reporter asked Tilden whom he considered the greatest French sculptor. Tilden replied: "I consider Rodin is the god almighty of the modern school! He makes every part of his work sing the same song as the whole."[29] Tilden never met Rodin.

The Bear Hunt

Trying to recall many years later how the idea for the *Bear Hunt* came to him, Tilden remembered that while he was in school, his attention was drawn to

> a wonderful plastic creation by leading German sculptor Max Klein, representing the captive Germanicus in the act of going into the arena entirely naked, and, with arms as powerful as bands of steel, throttling the lion to death. Both the man and the brute were on the floor; they were so interwoven that the lion apparently was powerless to use its claws. . . . I had this mental picture for a long time. The interesting problem would be to use the same scheme with an Indian and a bear . . . which would reflect an intensely American spirit.[30]

Pleased with his larger quarters consisting of a studio and three additional small rooms in a loft, Tilden began to work seriously on the idea of the group of figures that had been evolving in his mind for a long time. On September 6, 1891 he wrote: "I have been working more than a month on the group of Indians and Bears. It is nine feet from back to top and five feet across the face view. There are five figures in the group."[31]

When Tilden had finished his first sketch of the bear group, he learned from a friend that there was a similar work in the zoological gardens of Paris by Emmanuel Fremiet. Tilden hastened to check this out and found "such was the case, a caveman and a bear being shown standing breast to breast, the man wilting in the killing grasp. My Indian and bear present a full front, both in so full a vigor that Who wins: must forever be a question in the spectator's mind."[32] Tilden finished the group. It was cast in bronze and accepted in the Salon of 1892.

It was in the same year that Joaquin Miller, the poet of the Sierra Nevada, wrote a long extravagantly flowery article in praise of Tilden for a Bay Area Sunday newspaper:

> The new Michael Angelo . . . now in Paris. . . . This young man, not-withstanding the allurements of the Louvre, the tempting forms of beauty there, heroic, pathetic, terrible, in all attitudes indeed that appeal to the human heart, has been steadily and stubbornly true to his own land. . . . Shall I tell you of his struggles, his trials, his battle for bread? No. . . . It is enough I am privileged to record his triumphs; his three great works, all entirely American, and in line with our own prowess and daring, The Ball Player, The Tired Boxer, The Grizzly Bear, these attest his triumphs; his courage, his pride, his love of his own land. Let us glory in his victories, heal his wounds, and forget his hard, lone and forlorn fight. God sealed his lips in everlasting silence. It would be sacrilegious for me to say more than to shout his praise and say over and over again how much we love and honor him for his loyalty and his genius.[33]

About this time, Tilden sent several of his charcoal sketches to the California School for the Deaf for display in the art room. He also sent the director, Dr. Wilkinson, a gift of an oil portrait sketch of himself painted by Nestor Varveres, a rising young Greek artist studying in Paris. (Whereabouts of the painting is unknown.)

Method of Work

Tilden did no new modeling in Paris in the fall of 1892. He was too busy writing an article "The Art Education of the Deaf" to be presented at the World Congress of the Deaf in Chicago the following spring; also, he wrote an article regarding his own methods of working in his studio.

The malleable clay was a natural medium of expression for Tilden who continuously expressed himself in action. "The ideology underlying art and the sign method are exactly the same," wrote Tilden. "I see pictures mentally and think in gesture."[34] A single swift stroke of the thumb could be the triumph of the day. At first, he made a small clay model referred to by him as "a sketch"—a maquette—about twelve inches high. Tilden said: "The sole object [of the sketch is] to see how the parts of the figure or figures look in relation to each other. . . . They must be so huddled together that a downward stroke of a sword cannot pass between the figures without lopping off a head or limb."[35] Next, he made a larger clay model about one third the size of the finished work. After adjusting this model for perhaps two or three months, Tilden would be ready to begin the full-scale clay model. For this stage he used a turning table with an iron support strong enough to hold up a clay figure, six feet tall. On this support, brace iron strips were fastened, with bits of wood tied with wires, to hold the wet clay as the figure was built up. This build-up usually took several months, and it was necessary to keep the clay moist. Now came the finishing touches—the beauty, charm, poetry, fire—which Tilden said determined whether the artist was a master or not.

The process of changing a clay figure to a plaster figure was done by professional plaster moulders.

Casting the plaster figure into bronze was done in a foundry. Tilden mentions that his figures were made with sand casts and not by the lost wax method in the foundry. Tilden wrote: "Of course, from the beginning to the end of the process, you will have to overlook the work. . . . Next comes the chiseling and rasping to remove the uneveness of the surface. . . . Then comes the tinting of the surface. You can have the yellow bronze as it is, and leave it to the weather to put its mellow touches on it in the course of a few years. Or you can give any color to the bronze. The workmen can make it look 1000 years old, to order. . . . Each figure will have to be cast separately, and afterwards be united."[36]

In addition to his writing, Tilden prepared several of his works for the Chicago World's Columbian Exposition, commemorating the 400th anniversary of the discovery of America. He was appointed as a European juror of sculpture for the exposition. The *United States Constitution* arrived early the following spring to transport the works of art from Europe to the United States. Included on the frigate were Tilden's *Bear Hunt, Tired Boxer, Young Acrobat,* and the original plaster of the *Baseball Player.*

"Expansion of the American West," the theme of the exposition, marked the time when the West was acknowledged as part of the United States. A historical account of the Exposition states: "Those who have drawn their chief inspiration from Nature and life on this continent furnish some of the strongest and most original work that has been seen in the Exposition. . . . Mr. Tilden's Indian *Bear Hunt* is a fine monumental group."[37]

Tilden apparently felt the expense was too great and did not attend the Chicago Exposition—a keen disappointment for him. The hope of selling the *Bear Hunt* was uppermost in Tilden's mind. But economic clouds were gathering on the nation's horizon resulting in a financial panic—the worst in twenty years. The blow fell for Tilden in September, 1893, when the last communication he was to receive from Brown arrived: "I enclose Sterling Draft 15 ($75). This will be the last I shall be able to send you unless there is a very great change in the financial world."[38] Thus without warning, Tilden's resources were cut off. "My next move seemed clearly to pack up and go home, but then there was the clay group of the *Football Players* which . . . was already coming into shape as to be possibly a promising work." [This statuary included two figures—one, kneeling, bandaging the wounded leg of the other]. Later Tilden reminisced: "Should I abandon it to dry, crack, and subsequently lay an undistinguishable mass on the floor? I determined to hold on like grim death, even if I had to starve. . . . I had on hand some bronze replicas of my former works which I managed to dispose of at cost."[39] (These replicas, too, I have been unable to locate).

The isolation, frustration, and loneliness which Tilden experienced were eased when Granville S. Redmond, a younger deaf friend of long acquaintance, arrived in Paris from Berkeley to study painting. He stayed with Tilden. Redmond's studies were made possible by funds from the California School for the Deaf. For three years previous, he had won various honors at the Mark Hopkins Institute of Art where he had been enrolled as a student. In Paris, he immediately achieved recognition for his work in the Academy Julien, one of the leading art schools.

In the spring of 1894, Tilden exhibited the *Football Players* in the Salon. "The type of manhood presented is vigorous," said the critic, "but refined as befits unprofessional athletics."[40]

And so ended six years of rewarding study in Paris. Without the needed funds, Tilden had no choice. He sailed for home June 13, 1894. Before he left, he was given a farewell banquet by his French friends, and on arrival in New York he was honored with a reception by a host of more friends and admirers. Noting the beard he had grown while in Europe, these friends found him "a good deal changed in appearance but the same as ever in character."[41]

CHAPTER III

RETURN TO SAN FRANCISCO

San Francisco's Own

1894–1901

Fresh from Paris, Tilden arrived in San Francisco just in time to catch a glimpse of the final days of the California Midwinter International Exposition in Golden Gate Park before it closed July 4, 1894. This was San Francisco's first world fair—part of a renaissance of the arts in progress. Tilden found the city leaders awakening to the fact that the natural views were great but the buildings and streets were terrible. However, an era of artistic and architectural development had begun.

After the fair, civic leaders stepped forward with their new pride in the city and large financial contributions toward creating works of art for the city's beautification. Many citizens contributed their nickels, dimes, and dollars toward public subscription for monumental commemorative statuary. These men wanted statues of their heroes, and sometimes of themselves, to stand in public places in enduring bronze: they wanted their art also to express their confidence in a glorious future. "The purposes of art at the turn of the century were not those of the artists," Richard Mandel recently wrote, "but were those of all citizens who were to be inspired by confrontation with past examples of Man's nobility."[1]

The citizenry seemed obsessed with the idea of honoring the heroic accomplishments of the past decades. "The taste of the time," wrote William H. Hale in *The World of Rodin,* "demanded that a statue symbolize some noble human act drawn from history or mythology."[2] These desires, expressed by the grass roots of the people and supported by the generosity of the wealthy men and women in the community, attracted many artists. An artistic awakening occurred throughout the whole Bay

27

Area, a consciousness that the classical virtues of courage, industry, and righteousness should be expressed in visual form. "Sculpture found its true place as public monuments were erected under demand of new civic pride."[3]

Success in Europe was still the criterion by which artists were judged in San Francisco art circles. Tilden had achieved recognition in the art capital of the world, Paris. In the months ahead local newspapers used lavish headlines when they referred to him: "our foremost sculptor," "world famous sculptor," "one of the best known among the coterie of local prominent men," "a representative Californian," "the silent genius," and "Michelangelo of the West." Love, acceptance, and acclamation were showered upon him and healed the wound created by his involuntary leaving of Paris.

The Mark Hopkins Institute of Art

The San Francisco Art Association, founded in March 1871 by a group of artists and writers, exerted a powerful influence on the cultural growth of the city. This organization founded the School of Design in 1874, mostly from life-membership fees in the Art Association at $100 per person. The artist Virgil Williams was its first director; he was also one of the founders of the Bohemian Club in 1872. For many years the school flourished in quarters rented from the Bohemian Club on Pine Street.

Through the munificence of Edward F. Searles, who had married Mark Hopkin's widow, the Mark Hopkins palatial residence atop Nob Hill, which Searles inherited, was deeded to the Regents of the University of California in February 1893, "for the exclusive uses and purposes of instruction and illustration of the Fine Arts, Music and Literature."[4] The Regents endowed the San Francisco Art Association, which moved its School of Design into the fabulous spacious quarters commanding a panoramic view of the city, harbor, and bay. The mansion was named "The Mark Hopkins Institute of Art" in the spring of 1893.

Shortly after Tilden arrived in San Francisco in 1894, he settled in Virgil William's old studio situated in the abandoned Art Gallery of Woodward Gardens amusement park in the Mission district at 14th and Jessie Streets. In the fall, he was chosen to inaugurate modeling classes in the Mark Hopkins Institute—the first sculpture classes on the Pacific Coast.

When asked how he would teach, Tilden laughed: "I can talk to them in three languages [English, French, and the American Sign Language], but what I mean to do is to make them work."[5] His classroom at the institute was unique. For the first time a deaf man was instructing art students who could hear and speak. His unorthodox methods of communicating with pencil on paper and with pantomime exerted enormous influence on a young generation of Bay Area would-be sculptors. Also, he introduced live nude models, a novelty in California; the girls studied in the morning and the boys in the afternoon. "Modeling from a cast may be dreary monotony, but modeling from life has wide extremes of joy and woe. . . . The cheerful serenity of Douglas Tilden presided over all the struggle,"[6] wrote the San Francisco *Call*. Searles donated several fine plaster copies of classical sculptures including a colossal head of Michelangelo's *David*, Donatello's bust of *St. John*, Della Robbia's bust of a boy, and the torso of *Venus de Milo*.[7]

Tilden attracted attention in his unusual position. Above average in height, with broad shoulders and easy grace in movement, he was, as one reporter commented, "faultlessly dressed from the crown of his shiny hat to the tips of his patent leather shoes."[8] The reporter continued: "When one talks to him, his whole mental being becomes alert, his eyes seek those of the person with whom he is communicating. So trained is his conception that often before one has completely written a question or remark, he will signify dissent or agreement, he seems to be able to write upside down, wrong end first or any way he chooses."[9]

Tilden helped organize the Society of Arts and Crafts and was elected one of its seven directors. The goals of the group were "to bring together a body of men actively engaged in the arts of painting, sculpture, architecture, music and literature, that they might make a concerted action, influence the general taste, protesting against what is poor and unworthy, insisting upon a higher standard of art in public buildings, monuments and all public works."[10]

In the meantime, the bronze *Bear Hunt* arrived at the California School for the Deaf in Berkeley from Chicago. Tilden sent a drayman to pick up the statuary group to be delivered to the Mark Hopkins Institute for the spring art exhibit. Wilkinson, the superintendent of the school, refused to release it, stating that Tilden owed the school twenty-two hundred dollars for his education. Tilden was enraged; he acknowledged that he owed five hundred dollars, but insisted that he had not asked for the other seventeen hundred (even though he had signed three notes). His frustration and fury flamed into a bitter attack in the newspapers, denouncing Wilkinson and the Board of Directors. In turn, one of the Board of Directors, charged Tilden with ingratitude—"he is irascible and cantankerous—admitting such failings may be part of a young man's genius."[11]

During this time, James Duval Phelan, wealthy native son and patron of the arts, was gaining popularity in San Francisco as a political figure. However, "to him, the great conquering power of the world was art."[12] He commissioned Tilden to create a statuary group commemorating California's admission to the United States honoring the Native Sons of the Golden West. Tilden and Phelan dreamed of creating an Athens on the Pacific Coast. Phelan, a true Renaissance man, spent his personal fortune on the arts ordering several monuments to commemorate important events in his city's history.

Elizabeth Delano Cole

A new phase in Tilden's life began with a false rumor that appeared in d'Estrella's Itemizer column: "Douglas Tilden's name appears quite frequently in the society news. . . . It is rumored he is engaged to a wealthy hearing lady. Being received as a representative young man of California, he seems to have reached the top of the ladder, but we hope he has not forgotten his deaf friends."[13] There was no need for d'Estrella to worry. Tilden, shortly after, announced his intentions otherwise.

Just before Christmas of 1895, his engagement was announced to Elizabeth Cole, the deaf daughter of Leander G. Cole a wealthy entrepreneur of Oakland. "Bessie is a beautiful girl, lighthearted and vivacious. . . . It was at Berkeley that the lovers' romance began. Miss Cole became a pupil of Mr. Tilden, and he taught her apparently more than is prescribed by the regular course. When the teacher had completed his investigations in Europe and returned to California the tender friendship was renewed to blossom finally into an idyl of true love."[14]

Six months later, June 6, 1896, the wedding took place at the Cole residence, 1545 Webster Street, Oakland. "No more unique ceremony was ever performed," commented a reporter. "The talented sculptor read the pledge of the ceremony from a type-written copy and gave his promises in the language of the hand. The handsome bride, who also lacks the faculty of hearing, but can speak, read from a similar copy and gave her answer orally."[15] Willis Polk, a young architect, was best man.

The young couple joined the social life of the art circles, and the following spring, "Mr. and Mrs. Tilden attended the annual masquerade at the Mark Hopkins Institute of Art."[16] Other revelers laughingly chided them for their stern costumes portraying Miles Standish and Priscilla.

Two children were born to this marriage—a daughter, Gladys, and a son Willoughby.

About a year after the wedding, on a sunny afternoon of September 5, 1897, the new mayor James Duval Phelan spoke briefly at the unveiling of the *Admission Day* fountain. A large crowd gathered at the site at Market, Mason, and Turk streets as the young mayor stated that this statue was his gift to the city, commemorating California's admission to the Union. Tilden was introduced, with warm applause, as the sculptor who had created this work. An angel, the "lady on the top," was correctly surmised by all to be modeled from the artist's beautiful wife. As an allegory of history, the angel holds aloft an open book, as yet unwrit upon. On the cover is inscribed the date, September 9, 1850—the day California was admitted to the Union. Willis Polk designed the classic base and column that holds the angel. Inscribed on the base are U.S. Senator W. H. Seward's words: "The unity of our empire hangs on the decision of this day."[17]

Tilden had worked for several months on this statuary; his design had been selected over many others. William Dallam Armes wrote: "The boldness of design and excellence of execution would make the monument a noteworthy one in any city."[18] There was some criticism in the press because the figure of the prophetic young man held the flag in his left hand. And regret was expressed that the monument was erected so far up town and in an open space so restricted that the proximity of the surrounding buildings detracted from its impact. Tilden had suggested the foot of Market Street as an appropriate site.

The Overland Monthly

At about the same time another triumph was added to Tilden's fame, this time not as a sculptor, but as a literary figure. In August 1897, the *Overland Monthly* announced a competition for the best story of three thousand words, written by a scholar or teacher in a public school, or in a school receiving state aid, in California, Nevada, Oregon, and Arizona. More than sixty manuscripts were submitted, the authors remaining anonymous. In January came the announcement of the first prize, $100, to Douglas Tilden. The magazine printed: "The story displays the vigor seen in his sculpture—for most readers will recognize him as the young deaf-mute artist who has done so much for the cultivation of art on the Pacific Coast. It is entitled 'The Poverty of Fortune or Art Criticism in San Francisco.' It is illustrated by photographs of bas reliefs done in clay by Robert Aitken."[19]

In February, 1898, Tilden again appeared prominently in the *Overland Monthly*—this time as the central figure of a biographical article by Professor William Dallam Armes, director of the Greek Theater, University of California in Berkeley. "The leading citizens," Armes wrote, "now seem animated by a spirit akin to that that led the old Athenians to make their city renowned for its beauty. . . . Several monuments have been setup that should make forever impossible the monstrosities that formerly disfigured our streets." Armes summed up his lengthy article: "Considering Mr. Tilden's work as a whole it impresses one principally by its simplicity, directness and strength; its absence of mere sentimental prettiness. Knowing the antique well, he has revealed the grace, beauty and charm, in the seemingly commonplace and prosaic 'Art was given for that'."[20]

The success of the *Admission Day Monument* prompted Mayor Phelan to commission Tilden to create a model of the Spanish explorer Vasco Nunez de Balboa; it was to be placed at the western end of Golden Gate Park, looking out toward the Pacific Ocean. Tilden made the model, but it was never cast into bronze because the war with Spain made it seem untimely.

His Masterpiece

Tilden's best known work, his masterpiece, was the *Donahue Memorial Fountain,* now commonly called the *Mechanics.* A bequest of $25,000 for the erection of a public fountain, to be dedicated to mechanics, was left by James Mervyn Donahue in memory of his father, the industrialist Peter Donahue. The elder Donahue arrived in San Francisco in June 1849, and shortly thereafter opened a blacksmith shop. From this shop grew the

Union Iron Works—the Pacific Coast's first foundry. In it the first iron casting was made in California, and the first printing press was manufactured. Donahue was the first man to light the city of San Francisco with gas and the first to construct a street railway on the Pacific Coast. The foundry was situated on First Street, only a short distance from where the statuary group now stands.[21]

After the trustees of the Donahue estate had seen the unveiling of the *Admission Day Fountain,* they decided to commission Tilden to produce their memorial. Tilden made several clay sketches, but he was not satisfied. Then, one morning while walking down Mission Street, he saw a man operating a large level punch—a sight that, for him, was the solution of his problem. The trustees were skeptical when they saw the first sketch but Mayor Phelan won them over. Within six months Tilden's idea was translated into "what may fairly be termed the most unconventional work of sculpture in the United States," according to art historian Loredo Taft. "We may look upon its lawless composition and its ragged contour with the eye of criticism," Taft added, "but we can feel only admiration for the ardent and intrepid sculptor who wrought this wonder in those brief months. . . . Not only could no one but Mr. Tilden have made the *Mechanics Fountain,* but it could have been done in no other city than San Francisco. . . . An historic document, full of significance of time and place."[22]

The completed design includes five semi-nude men; two are holding the sheet of metal to be punched, while the three others work the arm of the lever press with demon-like zeal. At the base, an anvil, a propeller, and a locomotive driving wheel, symbolize the profession of Peter Donahue whose bas relief bust is on the front of the punch. Originally the inscription read: Omnia Vincit Labor, and streams of water gushed forth into a circular stone basin forty feet in diameter.[23] Willis Polk designed the classic pedestal.

The fountain part is long gone. The bronze group has been moved a few feet on several occasions to alleviate traffic or maintenance problems.

The graceful movements and gestures of the *Mechanics* create an art form in space, a continuous flowing rhythm of energy, in the hub of the city. The interplay of solid mass and space, the articulation of planes and curves, the sense of movement, create a unity of concept that belongs to the present day. And yet, the sublime expressions on the faces plunge one's imagery back in time to the figures of the Gothic cathedrals. The group stands now in a cathedral-like space with stone pillars of sky-scrapers reaching skyward, and colored glass windows reflecting all manner of things.

> steel meeting steel . . .
> soaring through the air . . .
> a man's masterpiece . . .
> but another tower of Babel?

These four lines from Bernard Bragg's "Another Tower of Babel," reflect so well the spirit of the *Mechanics*. Mr. Bragg is one of the founders and former director of the prestigious National Theatre of the Deaf.

The Football Players

The last statuary Tilden had created in Paris was cast in bronze in 1893, shipped to San Francisco, and shown at the Spring Exhibition of the San Francisco Art Association at the Mark Hopkins Institute in 1898; the *Football Players*. Phelan purchased the statue. Robert and Carol Sibley wrote in their treasury of tradition, *California Pilgrimage:* "Then Senator Phelan came upon the scene. He offered a beautiful football statue, the fine creative work of a blind [sic] sculptor named Tilden, to the university, Stanford or California, which would win the next two out of three games." California had never won a football victory over Stanford; she won 22–0 in 1898 and 30–0 in 1899.[24] Thus Tilden's *Football Players* today adorns the campus at Berkeley.

University President Benjamin I. Wheeler and Douglas Tilden chose the site at the southwest corner near the Life Sciences Building. On May 12, 1900, the day of the unveiling arrived. It was an auspicious day for the University of California: Mrs. Phoebe Apperson Hearst broke the ground for the president's house, the first phase of the Greater University. Many visitors attended. The graduating class of 1900 also celebrated their Class Day—going on the traditional pilgrimage. The finale was the unveiling of the *Football Players*. One of the speakers, on behalf of the student body said: "We are proud of this statue because of the sculpture, and because Douglas Tilden belongs to Berkeley . . . for it stands as an enduring monument of our first really college unity."[25] The statuary still stands in its original place, at times almost covered with shrubbery.

The Japanese painter Chiura Obata chose to include the statue in one of his celebrated paintings of the campus done in 1940. Obata poetically titled it, "Spring Rain, Football Statue," supplying the legend: "Lofty and mighty tradition of the past portraying students' victories against immeasurable odds inculcate new resolution and inspiration in today's students."[26]

Most critics felt that the *Football Players* was the most pleasing form from a sculpture point of view of the five major works Tilden produced in Paris. The lines and mass fitted in with the accepted tenets of sculptural form. However, the portrayed costume was viewed with surprise. It is that worn by English players whom Tilden sketched while visiting London. The ball is a combination of a rugby, a soccer, and a football. The player holding the ball is looking down toward the other kneeling figure who is administering a bandage to the standing player's leg.

The dining room of the Durant Hotel, Berkeley, shows a wall-sized oil canvas of the University of California Campus with the *Football Players* posed in the forefront. The painter, Jon O'Shanna, when asked if he knew Tilden and what was the reason for putting the statue of the *Football Players* in such a prominent position, replied: "No, I didn't know Tilden—there was no connection—I just liked it for its artistic value."

Unbeknown to Tilden, his friends in Paris entered the original plaster cast of the *Football Players* in the Paris International Industrial Exposition, 1900. It won a bronze medal. The Pan-American Buffalo Exposition of 1901 brought it to the United States and Tilden displayed it in their sculpture garden. Vandals damaged the plaster; I have not been able to find out what happened to the fragments.

Valentine Memorial and other Accolades

Sometime in the late nineties, Tilden created a bronze memorial, a shadowy draped, enshrined-figure, for the late Thomas B. Valentine family plot at Cypress Lawn Cemetery, San Mateo County. In 1851 Valentine who was described as "very industrious and economical" arrived from New York in San Francisco, where he founded a pioneer printing company (Valentine & Munson). However, he achieved his real glory as a real-estate promoter who increased his wealth by selling his famed "Valentine Scrip," which the United States Congress voted to have issued to him in lieu of a large grant of land he had purchased at Sonoma, because it was found that shortly after the purchase this rancho had previously been granted to a Mexican. Each certificate of location—or scrip—gave the owner the right to select 40 acres without homesteading obligations. These scrip certificates began to circulate at fantastic prices.[27]

Valentine was married twice, and when he died, October 27, 1896, in his Baldwin Hotel apartments, he left his widow—Jennie.[28] Inscribed on the bronze monument was his name, date of death, and the single Hebrew word—MIZPAH—which is translated: "The Lord watch between me and thee, when we are absent one from another." It was a long watch: Jennie did not join her husband in death until twenty years later.

This grandiloquent classic figure of grief stands eight feet high on a sloping hillside lawn, in a park-like setting, at the base of the San Bruno Mountain, surrounded by winding paths and many Victorian grave stones.

Also around the same time, Tilden designed a white marble bust of Father John Young, a professor at the University of Santa Clara, where it is now stored in the deSaisset Gallery on loan from the library.

In 1898 the San Francisco Art Association urged Mayor Phelan to appoint a committee to draft a comprehensive plan for the adornment of the city. Phelan appointed Tilden one of the nine members; they met at a Bohemian Club Luncheon—Tilden had become a club member in 1894 and was chosen the distinguished honorary member for 1895—to hear Phoebe Hearst announce a magnificent new project to make the city beautiful.

In the fall of 1899, the Regents of the University of California, under whose jurisdiction the Mark Hopkins Institute functioned, honored Tilden with a full professorship of Sculpture.[29] His influence as a teacher reached far and wide. Among his most successful pupils were: Robert I. Aitken, sculptor; Earl Cummings, sculptor and Park Commissioner; Edgar Walter, sculptor; Ernest Coxhead, architect; and John Bakewell, Jr., one of the architects for the new city hall, and Gertrude Boyle Kanna, sculptress.[30]

Tilden was a busy and happy man, a truly representative Californian. D'Estrella, proud of his old friend's accomplishments, acknowledged Tilden's prominence in the Itemizer column; "The name of the mute sculptor is so often mentioned in the different papers that it has become quite a household word to the art world as well as to the deaf."[31]

CHAPTER IV

CALIFORNIA'S HEROES ACCLAIMED

Monuments from the Oakland Studio

1901–1906

In the spring of 1901, major changes were set in motion for Tilden, when his father-inlaw, Mr. Leander Cole, died. Tilden's wife, Bessie, inherited the family home in Oakland.

As a young man, Cole had succumbed to a spell of gold fever, came to California, and remained about ten years without much success. But then he sailed on to New Zealand and success and fortune. He returned to Oakland in 1870. There he built his bride a handsome Victorian mansion near Lake Merritt fronting Webster and Franklin streets. Cole became an active councilman of Oakland, and it was said that, with a little more interest in politics, he might have been elected mayor. He and his wife frequently entertained Bessie's school friends from the California School for the Deaf in their home. In 1889 Mrs. Cole died, and 1896, Bessie and Tilden, after their marriage, moved into the Cole home so that she could care for her ailing father in his last years.[1] For Tilden, the move entailed an almost daily commute on the ferry across the bay to San Francisco to his teaching assignment and to his studio. Exhilarating sea breezes and grand vistas enlivened these otherwise tedious trips for him as did his warm friendship and commuting conversations with his friend, California-landscape painter William Keith.[2]

Shortly after Mr. Cole's death, the increased pressure of work from several commissions and the strain of almost daily commute to San Francisco, caused Tilden to resign his professorship at the California School of

Design, Mark Hopkins Institute of Art, and to move his studio to Oakland. The new, large, and well-lighted studio was situated in the carriage house of his home.[3]

National Competition

Now that Tilden had a more spacious studio and more available time, he wanted to expand his mature powers as a sculptor and decided to enter national competitions. For several months, he worked on a model for a competition for a *Ulysses S. Grant Monument* in Washington, D.C. His entry was the only one from California. There were thirty-six competitors.[4] The letter Tilden wrote accompanying the model to the committee of selection brings out some of his ideas in creating this work: "Gentlemen, I had carefully borne in mind the character and individuality of U.S. Grant, which are the essence of all American greatness and simplicity. . . . Great men, like great truths are simple . . . it is my belief that the war phases may best be illustrated by symbolism rather than realism."[5] According to the entry requirements, plans for improvement of the grounds around the White House had to be included. "I regret that, at this distance, it is impossible to make as comprehensive a study of this subject as I might, were I on the spot. I have never been in Washington. . . . I opine my model will harmonize with such a plan. . . . The impressions of the Avenues des Champs-Elysees of Paris may be thus surpassed."[6] He did not win the competition and it is said "he was not unduly disappointed as . . . he learned good things from the results." He donated the model to Gallaudet College, Washington, D.C., still the only existing liberal-arts college for the deaf.[7]

In 1902 architectural models competing for the award of a *William McKinley Memorial* in San Francisco, honoring the assassinated President of the United States, were exhibited at the Spring Exhibition of the Mark Hopkins Institute of Art. The committee of selection was not satisfied; they asked the competing sculptors, including Tilden, to try again, sculpture being preferred to architecture.[8] Robert I. Aitken, a former pupil of Tilden's, won this commission.

The city of Philadelphia also wanted a McKinley Memorial. Tilden submitted a model and it won accolades from the selection committee on its excellence, but it did not win the competition either. Tilden presented the plaster model to the Pennsylvania School for the Deaf in Philadelphia.

"It will be seen by thousands in the years to come," d'Estrella wrote, "who never saw such a work by a deaf man and may impress upon them the value of an art education to the deaf and be an inspiration to the pupils."[9]

The Gold Bear Hunt

In the spring of 1903, President Theodore Roosevelt made a sweeping visit to the West. On May 13, San Franciscans welcomed him to a gala day, with thousands of people in the streets to watch their president turn the earth for the erection of Aitken's *Memorial Monument* to Roosevelt's slain predecessor, William McKinley.

Early in the day President Roosevelt received a "costly souvenir of his visit," presented at the Native Sons of the Golden West Hall by former mayor James D. Phelan. The souvenir was an eight-inch gold replica of Tilden's bronze *Bear Hunt*. The design in standard paperweight form allegedly contained fifty ounces of California gold. In presenting the gift, Phelan said:

> We desire to give you some souvenir of this occasion, and we have evolved an idea which is here expressed in the precious metal of our native hills, designed by a native sculptor, Douglas Tilden, of whom we are proud, made by California artificers and wrought so deftly. Made of gold, we think it represents the state. . . . Why did we chose the bear? . . . the bear was—we have great respect for him—one of the earliest settlers . . . he died rather than submit to captivity . . . . He is put in the place of honor on our great State seal and flag.[10]

I accidentally discovered a front-page illustration of the statuette in the San Francisco Library's newspaper room, while laboriously viewing microfilms.[11] This led to several more months of search for the original. Finally, at the suggestion of the Registrar of the Office of the Curator, The White House, Washington, D.C.,[12] the gold replica was found to be at the Old Orchard Museum, Sagamore Hill National Historic Site, Oyster Bay, New York. The inscription on the front of the base reads: "To President Roosevelt from the Society of California Pioneers, The Native Sons of the Golden West, and the Native Daughters of the Golden West. San Francisco, California, May 13, 1903." The statuette was purchased by the

Theodore Roosevelt Association as part of the Roosevelt estate upon Mrs. Roosevelt's death in 1948. The estate was donated to the United States Government in 1963 and is administered by the National Park Service.[13]

Memorial to the California Volunteers

We often hear that each work of art shows the influence of its time and place. It tells us something about the emotions and skill of the artist who created it. But it can tell us also about the persons for whom it was made.

Today it is hard to comprehend the patriotic fervor that swept the community in 1898 as the soldiers prepared to sail out the Golden Gate for the Philippines in the war with Spain. "It happened that the first American troops, ever to leave the continent to fight an American war sailed, not from an eastern port, but from San Francisco. California's First Infantry on its way to the Philippines sailed May 23, 1898. San Francisco had never experienced such an emotional moment."[14]

The Spanish-American War, short and comparatively bloodless, brought the United States to the forefront in international politics. There was no draft; the men who fought were volunteers. San Francisco was the hospitality center of the United States for celebrations of fond farewells and victorious returns. When the troops returned from Manila, San Francisco went wild with enthusiasm. From the $65,000 raised by public subscription for a welcome-home reception, $25,000 was allocated to immortalize in bronze the volunteers. Tilden won the national competition for his design; it took him two years to bring his concept to fruition.

The bronze work, as it now stands, is sixteen feet high and ten feet long, mounted atop a granite base ten feet high. The statuary shows an American soldier, with a pointed gun in his right hand, and a sword in his left, standing over a fallen comrade in the throes of a death struggle. A dismounted cannon is close by. Above them is the goddess of war, Bellona, astride the winged horse Pegasus. The goddess is leaning forward thrusting out a sword with her right arm and holding a furled banner in her left.[15] The position of her body, encased in a Roman-warrior costume, is reminiscent of François Rude's *La Marseillaise* female figure on the Arc de Triomphe in Paris.

Later, replying to questions to how he had conceived the idea for this work, Tilden wrote on a pad to a reporter: "The basic thought is that the body dies, but the spirit goes on. When I start a subject I carry only one idea day and night for months. In modeling that group I continually said to myself: 'War is all horror and all confusion.' I had to do each figure two or three times over, the work occupying two years for modeling alone.''[16] Tilden, struggling to express how his ideas were translated into the actual three-dimensional form, continued writing: "The principal lines—the recumbent and the staggering man, the standard, Bellona herself and her accessories—are like rays diverging from a common center." He smiled, his hand gesturing approval of his thoughts, and wrote with a final flourish: "The bursting of a bomb!"[17] The reporter, then, slowly summed up his own thoughts: "The group has sort of scattering violence. It is unconstitutional, arresting, full of vigor."[18]

This statuary group later was to play a vital part in an even more dramatic event in the city's history.

A Monument for Oregon

In neighboring Oregon, the enthusiasm for the Spanish war volunteers culminated in raising $20,000 by public subscription for a bronze memorial. Tilden went by steamer to Portland and submitted a design. The selection committee accepted it unanimously.

The bronze figure, on top of a twenty-two-foot granite shaft, represents a volunteer in the field, full of life, charging forward, symbolizing service in the Philippines. Ernest Coxhead, San Francisco architect, designed the granite base and shaft.

On the day after the unveiling of the commemorative statue, the *Morning Oregonian* reported: "The gathering of people filled the entire block in the Lownsdale Square of Plaza Park; they came to pay tribute to their sons, fathers, friends, and sweethearts." One of the military speakers characteristically had this to say:

> The monument . . . is a milestone in the world's progress. It notes the first efforts to invade the domain of the Orient. Civilization does not go backward, neither does it much regard the feelings or wishes of peoples who oppose its sway. On this continent it crushed out the North American Indian to plant in his wilderness haunts the myriad homes and improved conditions of a beneficent civilization. Fifty years ago where we stand today was a wilderness tenanted by wild

beasts and untamed savages who disappeared before the advance of American civilization to make room for farms, factories, homes, schools, and churches, and humanity rejoices.[19]

Moving forward from one monumental artistic success to the next, Tilden's hard work and creative genius paid off in an unsolicited and unexpected honor in his election as a Fellow of the Royal Academy of Artists in London. "This society was formed in 1750," d'Estrella wrote, "and the membership includes about 2000 of the greatest men of Great Britain, King Edward being among the number. There were fifty American members, California having two."[20]

The Christmas number of the Mark Hopkins Institute's, *Review of Art,* 1903, reported that Douglas Tilden had completed a commissioned "architectural decoration" for the St. Louis World Fair. "It consists of a group of figures intended for the pediment over the Southern entrance of the Varied Industries building . . . this class of work with its severe limitations is so different from the style of freer subjects by which Mr. Tilden is more generally known in San Francisco."[21] Later, this work was awarded a commemorative gold medal. Tilden served on the jury of sculpture for this exposition.

Portrait medallions and tablets in bronze were much prized during this era. In the summer 1905, Tilden completed the bas-relief tablet portrait of the late University of California geology professor, *Joseph Le Conte,* for the Le Conte Lodge in Yosemite valley. Glamor surrounded the Le Conte's image since his son, Joseph N. Le Conte, had hiked into the high Sierra with President Roosevelt on his visit to the West. The Sierra Club paid five hundred dollars for the bronze casting; Tilden gave his services free in fond memory of Yosemite.[22] The younger Le Conte's sister-in-law, Susan Gompertz, one of the first teachers at the California School for the Deaf, was a friend of Tilden's.

A Commission for Los Angeles

In 1905, the *Stephen Mallory White Memorial* Association offered an award for a memorial in bronze to be erected in honor of U.S. Senator Stephen M. White near the Los Angeles Courthouse.

White, a San Franciscan by birth, opposed the declaration of the war with Spain in a masterpiece of oratory. His greatest achievement was "his tireless and eventually successful contest for the establishment of a free harbour at San Pedro.''[23]

Funds for the monument were raised in Los Angeles by public subscription amounting to more than $20,000. The competition was open to all American sculptors.[24]

In October 1905, the *Los Angeles Times,* noted that an "award of first premium for design, two hundred and fifty dollars, was made to Douglas Tilden, a San Francisco sculptor."[25]

Father Junipero Serra

Yet another commission was forthcoming. Phelan, who deeply believed in the powerful influence of art, during his three terms as mayor sponsored music, literature, and the arts in San Francisco. He was a native San Franciscan who, in his appeals to the citizens to beautify the city, led the way with generous gifts. He commissioned Tilden to create a monumental bronze likeness of Father *Junipero Serra,* the legendary founder of San Francisco.

Father Serra had a dream of establishing a settlement on the shores of San Francisco Bay to honor the founder of his order, St. Francis of Assisi, from whom the city gets its name. Illness prevented Father Serra from reaching his goal, but his friend, Father Francisco Palou, carried out his wishes. On June 29, 1776, he said the first mass under the shelter of hastily assembled branches, near the present site of Mission Dolores, to a small band of settlers from Mexico. This is the date San Francisco has used to celebrate its birthday.

Tilden completed the plaster statue of the Spanish padre, founder of the California missions, in March 1906. It stood more than nine feet high although the missionary was scarcely five feet. Archbishop P. W. Riordan, after viewing the plaster figure in the studio, declared it magnificent and raised his hand in blessing as he left Tilden's studio. *Serra* poses as a visionary father, with his right hand extended, planting the cross of Christianity upon California soil. The left arm is raised in benediction as the figure almost strides forward for the blessing. "I have represented the face thinned by hardships," wrote the sculptor, "but I decided to tone down the furrows a little, for you know, the outdoor air will darken the bronze after a while and unduly emphasize them. . . . It should be viewed only from below."[26] Time has rendered a lovely greenish patina.

Concern over Prejudice for the Deaf

Tilden, beyond his dedication to art, was driven by a deep concern for his deaf fellows. "Sculpture is not a trade or a craft; it is an art that has for its chiefest business the study of man."[27] And study man he did. He found the needed energies to work unceasingly for the advancement and improvement of the deaf which he thought could best be accomplished by bringing the deaf and the hearing together. He wrote: "The deaf were first treated with abhorrence, which could not be wiped out, except at the price of death; next they were allowed simply to vegetate; next they were pitied; next they became objects of professional interest. Today, at the beginning of the 20th century, I believe that I see indications that the deaf are beginning to be respected."[28] His creed was: "People must know us." "The deaf," he wrote, "should make themselves known to the hearing world. There cannot be one standard set up for the hearing and another for the deaf."[29]

On November 8, 1902, for the first time in the history of the deaf in California, a Social Club of Deaf Mutes gathered in San Francisco for a banquet "in an atmosphere of democracy." After the dinner, various speakers responded to the toasts concerned with education of the deaf. Dr. Wilkinson urged that the deaf be educated, "because it is a matter of safety and profit to the State, and makes the deaf happy and useful citizens." Tilden, one of the guest speakers, "excited deep emotions in those present with his happy faculty of making signs gracefully and in lucid style, becoming eloquent." Responding to the toast, "To the Deaf in Art," he asserted: "There is no field in the struggle of life which can do more for the deaf than art, to secure recognition from the public and through this to bring them upon a common footing, irrespective of class or clique."[30]

Tilden fought against society's prejudices held toward the deaf, prejudices that he attributed to ignorance. He thought these prejudices were enhanced by the growing trend toward oralism in deaf education, a trend to which he was bitterly opposed. He concluded his remarks about oralism in a paper read for him to a hearing group: "Its principle that the deaf should become part of the normal world, is correct, but in applying the principle the oralists succeed in hurting us. Their application of the principle is unpracticable, unnatural and even criminal."[31] He often emphatically stated, "The sign language is our language."

As a true deaf-awareness gesture, the Sunday edition of the *San Fran-cisco Call,* published a full-page illustrated biographical sketch about Tilden plus a long article written by Tilden, titled: "Deaf Mutes and the World of Pantomime." He wrote: "The deaf live in a world of their own: a world of pantomime, a world of eternal silence, totally unknown to the majority of hearing people. To every 2000 citizens there is perhaps one deaf mute." He contended that most people thought that because a man was mute he must also be an ignorant being, but, he added: "in reality the gray matter of the mute is of just as fine a fiber as is that of a hearing man."[32]

Tilden characterized the deaf as having utter faith in hearing people and high regard for the authority of the newspaper; in other words, a complete dependence on the judgment of hearing friends. He repeated his belief that one area in which the deaf could become successful was art, and agreed with the unnamed professor from a nearby university, who said: "Fearful as your deprivation may be, your true means of expression is preserved you, not of intellectual ideas through words, but of aesthetic ideas through form—you can see at least."

California Association of the Deaf

A growing interest among the deaf themselves for further organization led to a memorable date in the history of the deaf in California—October 22, 1905. It was a preliminary meeting of nine deaf men and women in the studio of Tilden to consider the organization of an Alumni Association of the California School for the Deaf. There was much discussion about the necessity for the deaf uniting for their common good: the main issue was whether the group should be limited to graduates of the California School for the Deaf or include the deaf at large in the state. Many deaf residents in California had received their education elsewhere. Tilden was the right man to spearhead the formation of the group and assume the leadership.[33] At the second meeting, it was decided: "A state association was prefera-ble to an Alumni association—hence it is the California Association of the Deaf."[34] Tilden drafted the constitution and by-laws. One of the first alterations in the Constitution was to substitute "the deaf" for "deaf mutes" in the wording.[35] Later, in 1909, Tilden was elected President. But in the following years long-standing personality conflicts erupted, tempers flared, and the association disbanded in 1913. A short time later it was reorganized but Tilden did not participate.

An important catalyst for deaf awareness was generated when a secret fraternal national organization, the Order of the Americans, included the deaf as a separate, but equal, chapter in their organization. In an article that Tilden wrote for the *Deaf-Mutes' Journal,* he used the headline: "Old Time Chinese Wall of Exclusiveness Broken Down."[36] The chapter's first annual banquet at the California Hotel, San Francisco, brought together thirty-five deaf and twenty-three hearing persons on the cold wet evening of February 21, 1906. The flying fingers of introductions and reunions added to the gaiety. There were fragrant flowers and soft lights in the dining room, the ladies and gentlemen were festively attired, some in full evening dress, and the menu left nothing to be desired.

Menu

Eastern Oysters Half Shell

Consomme en Tasse

Olives   Salted Almonds

Shrimp Salad, Mayonaise

Fried Fillet of Sole, Tartar Sauce

Pommes Parisienne

Tenderloin of Beef aux Champignons

Orange Sherbet

Roast Chicken au Cresson

Green Peas

Vanilla Ice Cream   Assorted Cakes

Camembert Cheese

Fruits

Cafe Noir

Douglas Tilden, charming and gracious, presided as toastmaster over the evening's festivities.[37]

A few weeks later, April 14, 1906, Tilden left Oakland to finish his monumental bronze in Portland, Oregon. He did not realize that he would never see the same San Francisco again.

CHAPTER V

AFTER THE INFERNO, 1906

The Rebuilding

1906–1914

"Poor San Francisco! A city, formerly gay, rich, and peaceful, it's now only a mass of ruins," wrote Tilden, in French, to a friend in Paris, three weeks after the catastrophe of the earthquake and fire, which struck on April 18, 1906, at 5:12 A.M. "The fire . . . destroyed the city down to the bare ground. Imagine 25km of smoking ruins! . . . . Two of my works are still standing. I was making 50,000 fr. a year, but alas sculpture will be dead 10–15 years."[1] Tilden was prophesying the end of his opportunities. The commission for the *Junipero Serra* statue was to be his last for a monumental figure.

Because of his hearing impairment or of his isolation in his work in Oregon, Tilden did not know about the disaster for twenty-four hours after it occurred until he saw the glaring headlines of a newspaper. He recalled later that his anxiety, when he found out, "was more poignant still than the earthquake itself, for the telegraph was completely disrupted and it was impossible to get news of my family."[2] He felt relief and deep gratitude to find that his family and his studio had escaped unharmed when he arrived home a few days later. But his house had suffered severe damage. All chimneys had collapsed. Besides, several small clay models were broken in the studio.

The *Mechanics* and the *Admission Day* statuary, in San Francisco, survived as the city around crumbled: but the *Tired Boxer* was destroyed in the holocaust at the Olympic Club.

Shortly after Tilden arrived home in Oakland, he wrote to Phelan expressing sympathy for Phelan's heavy losses of his home and properties, and vowing: "I am ready to roll up my sleeves for a new and greater San Franciso. . . . Junipero has not a scratch, tho it moved about 3 inches." Then he expressed his thoughts that "it will be cheering to the people to have *California Volunteers* set up among the ruins without further delay. Shall I tell Chicago to ship [the Volunteers] at once?"[3] Phelan suggested they wait a month pending the Supervisors' decision on plans for a new Civic Center.

California Volunteers Group Spurs on Restoration

Four months later, August 12, 1906, "under the fairest of California skies in the bright sunlight of Sunday afternoon," a glorious parade moved up Van Ness Avenue from the Presidio to the spot near Market Street where three thousand citizens gathered to witness the unveiling of Tilden's monument dedicated to the *California Volunteers*. A thrill went through the crowd as they watched former Mayor Phelan pull the cord that let the flag drop from the bronze figures as the band played "The Star Spangled Banner." Mr. M. H. deYoung, civic leader, representing the citizens committee, stood by.[4]

George C. Pardee, governor of California, accepted the gift on behalf of the two million people of the state. The chairman of the day introduced James F. Smith, governor general of the Philippines, who spoke: "The war with Spain brought much sorrow and sacrifice, but who will say it was not a preparation which made men smile in the face of ruin on the 18th of April and in the instant of crushing disaster gave them courage to set themselves to restore the fortunes of a lifetime shattered in a moment. . . . Let the monument to it be a city more splendid, more glorious, more beautiful."[5]

The chairman called for Tilden to come forward to the speaker's stand. He did not—because he was modest or perhaps he did not hear the call. Two days later, he wrote Phelan: "It was the prettiest unveiling I ever witnessed. San Francisco stands in the face of the world in the attitude of a woman who is in tatters and yet has enough elegance to stick a jewel in her hair. That is splendid, is it not? The eloquence of the unveiling was more than equal to the idea I had tried to express in bronze."[6]

On the first of September, the "Forum," a group of deaf citizens in Oakland, gave a banquet to honor Tilden for the success of the *Volunteers* monument. The toastmaster summed up their feelings that "Tilden's buoyancy of spirits and energy have brought not only success and prosperity to himself but that they have also done much toward educating the hearing concerning the capacities of the intelligent deaf."[7]

Tilden's studio became a haven for artists who had suffered severe losses in the disaster. Haig Pattigan, sculptor, resumed his work there. Several deaf men were employed as carpenters. Six months after the earthquake, Tilden wrote Phelan: "I have not crossed the bay since the unveiling day. . . . These are times to try men's souls."[8]

A few months later, the San Francisco *Call* decided to hold a beauty contest to offer some relief from the strain of suffering and heartaches following the catastrophe to the city. In this lighter vein, Tilden was drafted to serve on the board of judges—a task he enjoyed. The judgments were made entirely from photographs—many hours were spent studying the pulchritude. At the request of the *Call*, Tilden wrote out his opinion with scientific seriousness:

> Beauty is variety in unity and unity in variety, and art is the highest idealization by the human mind of that beauty. This variety in unity and unity in variety that we would attempt to idealize in painting or sculpture, we also attempt to find in its greatest perfection in the human face. Besides the regularity of features conforming to the most acceptable canons of art, I consider these requisites paramount in passing on the beauty of the women whose photographs were placed before us. Esprit, without which no women can be said to be really beautiful; wellbredness, which is another name for refinement; and health, which is inseparable from the balmy influence of our glorious skies.[9]

Also in 1907, Tilden made an erotic clay model, titled "*Golden Gate.*" Two entwined figures, with the upper bodies those of a man and a women and the lower parts those of writhing serpents, embrace high on the crest of a wave; sea gulls and sea lions are watching.

Junipero Serra

After the earthquake, the unharmed plaster cast of *Junipero Serra* was shipped to Chicago for bronze-casting at the American Bronze Foundry, and Tilden visited Chicago for the first time after thirteen years. The cast was widely acclaimed in the Chicago press and the *Monumental News*.

The sun seemed to shine always on the dedication ceremonies of Tilden's statuary. On November 17, 1907, a beautiful day in San Francisco, a large crowd gathered at Academy and Court Drives, near the M. H. de Young Memorial Museum in Golden Gate Park to witness the unveiling of *Father Junipero Serra*. "Jolly Fellow" wafted on the breezes from the nearby band shell.[10] Tilden had written earlier to Phelan requesting that the statue be placed south of the Ferry Loop: "Lift up your heart, lift up your heart! That will be the language that the bronze speaks to thousands passing by."[11]

Edgar Mathews, architect, designed the base. The inscription date on the west side, October 9, 1776, refers to the official founding date for Mission San Francisco de Assisi (Mission Dolores), the oldest building in the city.

Around this time Tilden designed a fifteen-inch medallion of *Junipero Serra* with praying hands. This design was used for the historical landmark #128, the granite *Junipero Serra Cross* which stands on the landing spot of Junipero Serra at Monterey, California. The plaster cast of the medallion later won a gold-medal award at the Alaska-Yukon Exposition, 1909, in Seattle. The bronze cast of this medallion has recently been installed in the courtyard of the new museum in Mission Dolores.[12] Tilden presented the *Serra* likeness to Willis Polk who later bequeathed it to the Mission.

Stephen Mallory White Statute

The clay model of U.S. Senator Stephen M. White also escaped the earthquake. Tilden continued to work on it and in March of 1907 a committee from Los Angeles arrived at the Oakland studio to inspect the work for approval. It was judged a remarkable likeness.[13] This plaster model was also shipped to Chicago for bronze casting. Architect Ernest Coxhead was selected to design the base.

The dedication ceremonies of the *Stephen M. White Memorial* statue on December 11, 1908, in Los Angeles, surpassed anything San Francisco had seen. Twenty thousand people attended the parade leading to the dedicatory site in front of the court house.[14] "The unveiling of sculpture became a peculiarly Victorian event," wrote James M. Goode, curator of the Smithsonian Institute, recently. "The dedication of a statue often resulted in the closing of all businesses, with crowds of 20,000 or more attending the band concerts, parades, and marathon speeches that accompanied nineteenth—century dedications."[15]

The Los Angeles *Daily Times* printed almost two full pages of illustrated copy, headlined, "Laurels of Great Love Placed on Beautiful White Memorial."[16] The editorial column, of the day before, was titled, "California's Greatest Native Son."[17]

Leading citizens were seated on the platform for special guests. Lieutenant-Governor Warren R. Porter represented the state of California. Other seats were occupied by prominent federal, state, and city officials. Mrs. Douglas Tilden was given a place of honor. Former governor Henry T. Gage, long-time personal and professional associate of Senator White, delivered the main speech. School children sang "America the Beautiful." At last, the bronze heroic-size likeness, representing Senator White in a characteristic pose of speaking with his right hand outstretched and the left in his pants' pocket, was unveiled.[18]

During a seven-year period, contributions had been collected throughout the United States amounting to $25,000 for the *White* memorial.[19]

Fifty years later, the Los Angeles *Times* again had occasion to report on the statue: "The Father of Los Angeles Harbor—two tons of Los Angeles and California history—was moved yesterday from the site of the old red stone County Courthouse to a new home."[20] Today it stands in front of the Los Angeles County Law Library at 1st and Hill Streets.

McElroy Memorial Fountain

Tilden's next triumph was a series of bronze inserts into a monument in Oakland, a fountain to honor John Edmund McElroy, a former Oakland city attorney.

"Thousands of Oaklanders Gather at Classic *McElroy Memorial Fountain*," headlined the Oakland *Tribune* the day after the dedicatory ceremonies of September 17, 1911. Mayor Frank K. Mott delivered the address at Lakeside Park within view of Lake Merritt and a fleet of white-winged sailing craft. The idea for the memorial originated with James P. Edoff, president of the Oakland Park Commission, to honor McElroy's unselfish devotion to the city of Oakland. McElroy supported the development of the park and boulevard system of Oakland; it was said that when he was city attorney "Oakland began to show signs of life and awakened from its long sleep.''[21] A part of the money for this park memorial was raised by subscription from McElroy's friends.

The *Tribune* described the fountain in detail: the center marble bowl was ''a single piece of quarried Georgian marble, eight feet in diameter, weighing three tons. The water flows over the rim like a veil of silver.''[22] Walter D. Reed designed ''This most beautiful fountain on the Pacific Coast.''

At the dedicatory ceremonies it was announced that the fountain would eventually be decorated by twelve bronze inserts, typical of California life, ''designed by the well known sculptor Douglas Tilden.'' The cost was to be $2000, contributed by family and friends of the deceased.[23] The greenish-bronze bas-reliefs are in situ at the present time. However, I have been unable to find out when they were cast, where they were cast, or when they were attached to the marble panels. An isolated note in d'Estrella's ''Itemizer'' in December 1912 states that in the private annual exhibition of the Bohemian Club artists and sculptors, in San Francisco last month, was an allegorical group in plaster of *''The Twelve Stages of Man,''* by Douglas Tilden, designated for the McElroy Fountain.''[24] The iconography as it stands now, depicts twelve separate scenes from babyhood to death.

Clay Models, Ug

In the following year, Tilden made several small-scale models in clay which included three memorials, one for *General Barnett* of San Jose, one for *John Bidwell* of Chico, and one for the *Donner Party* at Donner Summit; he also made a model of a fountain for Los Angeles. He awaited action from the various committees but funds were lacking and the monuments were never commissioned. D'Estrella, after a visit to the studio, commented, ''Some of them ought to be immortalized in bronze or marble on a much larger scale. . . . They would rank among the masterpieces of sculpture.''[25]

D'Estrella's favorite was a model of the *Abbe de l'Epee* ''which commemorated the memory of the man who unselfishly sacrificed his life in the cause of the deaf. The good abbot is standing on the middle of a horizontal, oblong pedestal; on one end of it a human being in fetters represents Darkness, on the other end another being free of bondage represents Light.''[26] This model is now in a private family collection.

Tilden also completed a model of *"Joaquin Miller Embarking for Valhalla,"* a proposed monument to the poet of the Sierra. This was described as being created "for the park across the street from the new city hall in Oakland."[27] It was not used.

In August of 1913, the Bohemian Club of San Francisco sponsored a stage play, "The Fall of Ug: A Masque of Fear" by Rufus Steele, a member. It was performed by a company of club members at the Bohemian Grove, among the giant redwoods in Sonoma County, California. Printed comments of the production explained that Ug was the God of Fear, and his fall was brought about by understanding.[28] Tilden spent many happy hours designing the overpowering colossal fabricated figure of *Ug* which collapsed at the appropriate moment in the drama.

California's Hall of Fame

On October 27, 1914, the Native Sons of the Golden West dedicated their "Hall of Fame" in their building on Mason Street. The ceremonies included the unveiling of thirteen art glass panels depicting native-born Californians who had won international distinction and fame in the arts, literature, science, and drama. The committee of selection included James D. Phelan, Louis F. Byington, and Henry G. W. Dinkelspiel.

From the scores of names submitted they selected Mary Anderson, actress; Sybil Sanderson, opera singer; Gertrude Atherton, author; Maude Fay, opera singer; Douglas Tilden, sculptor; Ernest Peizotto, painter and writer; Jules Pages, painter; David Warfield, actor; Jack London, author; David Belasco, playwright; Dennis O'Sullivan, opera singer; Professor John J. Montgomery, scientist and inventor; and Richard Walton Tully, author and playwright.[29]

This honor brought with it some of the pervading emotions in which Tilden was to find himself increasingly engulfed. He poured forth his feelings in a letter to Phelan:

> Yes, I was present at the interesting ceremonies of the unveiling of the art glass windows. It is a high gratification to me to be enrolled among men and women whom your committee think deserve well of the state and I thank you in your capacity as Chairman . . . sad reflections, all others have left the state, only exception was myself. I have camped right here only to find that what I imagined twenty years ago

is after all an illusion. Whereas I thought that the demand for my services would not only grow but also be continuous, I have in truth done but little these last few years and sold much less.[30]

The art glass panels are now covered with dark green paint; the Hall of Fame has become a local cinema.

Panama-Pacific International Exposition

The rebuilding of San Francisco culminated in the Panama-Pacific International Exposition of 1915. Although San Francisco, in her haste "to get on with it," did not become architecturally a dream city, the grand design and sculptural embellishment of the Exposition grounds created a temporary "vision of jewelled splendour." The leading sculptors of the United States were invited to display their talents. Stirling Calder of New York was in charge of general supervision of ornamentation. Tilden worked for many months on a design called *Modern Civilization* to be placed in the plaza in front of the Palace of Machinery. In the San Francisco *Bulletin,* he described this work:

> The design consists simply of a row of five upright figures, about 17 feet tall, the titles being respectively Valor, Morality, Truth, Imagination and Industry. The base is about 28 feet long. At one end Valor, in the commanding attitude stands spear in hand, while at the other end Industry, holding a sledge and a plowblade inscribed with the words "Labor omnia vincit."
>
> The figures are all nude. Truth is throwing backward the drapery in the familiar attitude of Venus rising out of the waves or Ariadne emerging out of the mist. Imagination is leaning against a treetrunk, in a pensive mood, and Morality is modestly flinging a robe around her chaste body.
>
> The effect of the whole composition is that of unique squareness which will harmonize with the expanse of the Palace of Machinery, in front of the main entrance.[31]

A disagreement ensued regarding the completion of this colossal work, and on January 23, 1915, Tilden wrote Phelan about it: "I am sorry to tell you my monument *Modern Civilization* which was ordered for the Exposition is not likely to be erected, as the Fair is too poor to pay for it."[32] Indeed, the Fair took place without Tilden's monument.

CHAPTER VI

THE LEAN YEARS

Sculpture Declines

1916–1925

In the next decade, threatening changes occurred in the world of Douglas Tilden, over which he had no control. The United States went to war; the era of the wealthy art patron, at least for Tilden, ended; and the public demand for costly monumental statuary diminished.

Tilden's deafness prevented him from active participation in the war. He lost Phelan's financial and moral support when Phelan was elected U.S. Senator, moved to Washington, and turned his interests and energies to the war. Tilden's increased isolation, in his silent world, lessened his opportunities to communicate with other artists about ideas emerging on the world art scene—commemorative and memorial statues were no longer a fashionable public gesture.

Changes in the World of Art

"Between 1876 and 1915," wrote Wayne Craven in *Sculpture in America*, "America created a unique gilt-edged society that was both crassly materialistic and loftily idealistic; and it demanded of its art a bold naturalism that would be compatible with its materialism and an idealized imagery that would reflect its destiny, its aspirations and its enormous pride and confidence."[1] Monumental commemorative and memorial bronze statuary filled those needs.

However, during the first two decades of the 20th century, the outlook of many artists slowly changed from representational conventions of expressions to a more personal vision; the new ideas stemmed primarily from scientific exploration and invention; abstract nonrepresentational sculpture emerged. According to Craven: "It became obvious that the United States, along with most of the Western world, had recognized the necessity for a new art to express her joys, sorrows, and beliefs."[2] However, Craven added, "there continued to be, the generation of men who met head-on a revolutionary 'modern art' that they could not understand and therefore could not absorb."[3] Tilden fitted somewhat, but not entirely, into this group. The confrontation between the two viewpoints continues to this day.

Many art historians writing about Western art do not include the art of the Western United States in their considerations. But in referring to the growing consciousness of all that is American, Patricia Broder, in her *Bronzes of the American West,* introduces the idea that "On every level—historical, environmental, spiritual, and ethnic—the bronze sculptures of the American West are the most permanent expression of America's national heritage. . . . Bronzes of the West are America's most unique form of sculpture."[4]

However, in the decade after the earthquake many artists left California, and New York became the center for creative activities in the arts. Many artists moved to Europe.[5] Tilden was a Californian. His roots, his work, his home, and family were all centered in the state he loved, and it was hardly possible for him to move on to the bigger arena of the East Coast. Yet, he wrote to his friend Phelan: "Sculpture is about dead here."[6]

With dwindling opportunities for sculpture, Tilden rekindled an earlier ambition. "I am determined more than ever to break into literary California," he wrote to his friend, the writer Ellas S. Mighels. "At any rate, the hankering has to be gotten rid of like a cold."[7] She carefully read and made suggestions for his autobiographical manuscript "Dummy." In one letter to her Tilden wrote: "Truth is important. Am I conceited? The public ought to like to know that—in the next century—when it looks over my monuments. . . . The word 'Dummy' . . . it is your vernacular. I think the title is picturesque—catchy."[8]

Jack London was also his friend. A copy of the Tilden manuscript was found on London's bedside table on the day London died; corrective notes had been added. Ten days before London's death, Tilden and two deaf friends visited the writer at his famed Valley of the Moon home in Sonoma. Photographs were taken with London. Tilden presented to him the erotic clay model, *"Golden Gate"* which Tilden had finished years before. He inscribed it: "To Mr. and Mrs. Jack London, November 12, 1916." In 1969 this statuette was cast in bronze and is now on display in The Oakland Museum. The manuscript was never published to my knowledge.

Attempts to Return to Teaching

After the failure of his literary efforts, Tilden turned once again to his alma mater, the California School for the Deaf, and asked the superintendent, Mr. L. E. Milligan, for an appointment to work there. He emphasized that the San Francisco fire had been hurtful, luxuries had to stand aside, hard times followed, and finally, "We are in the throes of a world wide conflict. The *Junipero Serra* monument was the last I erected and that was ten years ago. I will need a half day to myself to continue my literary or art work and I imagine that at the same time, I can serve you well."[9] But Tilden was not employed at the school.

On June 29, 1917, the Twenty-first Meeting of the Convention of American Instructors of the Deaf was held in Hartford, Connecticut, and Tilden was asked to participate in the Art Section of the five-day meeting. He was unable to attend but sent a paper "The Value of Art to the Deaf." In it he stressed that "art can be a means of education"[10] and that all schools for the deaf should include the teaching of art. "Art will arouse his [the deaf child's] facilities to such a degree that he will speak out his soul through it with more success than is possible by any other means. . . . An artist will often see vividly . . . and yet have to brood over the chaos of his imaginings before he can shape them into a creation. This principle of vision is the same in literature as in architecture, painting, sculpture—in philosophy and mathematics as well. . . . Imagination is simply the power of forming images."[11]

In regard to method, Tilden thought that drawing was of first importance: "Make the child draw from objects before him. . . . Teach the child to work rapidly and playfully. While learning to draw the pupil is led on to get interested in higher and better things—to perceive what constitutes grace, which we know as the principle of beauty."[12]

Tilden had long held the belief of "a beneficial connection between art and our language of image writing in the air." He admonished the audience at the convention: "Always bear in mind Aristotle's assertion that the most intellectual quality is the power to recognize familiar objects (which power is true of the children)" and commented further on the usefulness of art education: "It will be useful when applied to trades or other activities of life, and a boy will certainly be a better carpenter, a better engineer, and even a better editor, or minister for having taken lessons in the art department."[13]

Then Tilden pleaded: "I beg that you deal tenderly with the gifted pupil as you would with some uncommon and yet glorified creature, for his lot will be to see vividly, feel strongly, and suffer deeply."[14]

In conclusion, Tilden wrote: "Success in art arises from no one condition; and the pale vision-seer, deaf, silent, and full of resentment against his fate may yet surmount his limitations, so that the delighted world will say, 'The schools for the deaf are an honor to the land, and their teachers are men and women who serve humanity well.' I believe the use of signs . . . is a real assistant in art education as it is in education in general. Let us work on."[15]

In February 1918, continuing personal and family problems brought another plea to the principal of the School for the Deaf. "I am to move out of my studio," Tilden wrote, "and that gives me very much of a lost feeling. . . . May I ask again if there is any prospect of going to your school?"[16] The reason for his move is alluded to in a letter to Phelan in Washington, D.C.:

> I thank you more than I can express for the check, which by the way, I needed badly. . . . I was required to vacate at once. I moved into a rear room of the building where I staid in the state of quasi-resistance till I could cast the clay model in plaster and get my bearings. I am now in a little shed in the rear of the above address. . . . If you can repeat the remittance, I can make the shed more useful and habitable. . . . I long ago slept on a couch by the side of the wet statues of the *Baseball Player* and the *Tired Boxer* as I am now again sleeping in the midst of my sculptures. . . .
>
> I would like to go on in my profession. It is understood that I personally am nothing, I belong to the world. I am in my prime; I am dumb but full of speech and I want to give utterance to many things. I think my latest design would make a great monument and increase Market Street's fame. But it is up to the world to furnish me with means for doing so. I cannot create both ideas and means. As human affairs seem everywhere to be upset, I will after all have to take up some other line of work and I am willing to do so."[17]

With the war finally over, Tilden wrote to Superintendent Milligan: "It would be well to join an institution, instead of continuing an institution by myself. We seem to be facing more stupendous problems than those with which we grappled during the war. Art is reviving; the enthusiasm is there, but the financial side of the matter may continue to bother us."[18]

But his repeated attempts to seek employment at the California School for the Deaf ended in frustration. Deaf teachers were no longer employed. Tilden poured out his bitterness to his old friend Phelan: "It has turned into a pure oral school. This is a wicked plan as the oral system is good for only exceptional pupils, and the rest is liable to be reduced to more or less idiocy as the result of experimentation. The oral system originates in Germany as against the sign method which is French, and the work of the oralists is pure and simple German propaganda."[19]

His desperate desire to return to the school would not be quenched. He asked Phelan to write to the California School for the Deaf Board of Directors to plead for him, ending the note, "I cannot draw on your friendly benevolence much longer. Thirty dollars a month is a mere pittance—just enough for food with nothing for fuel or light or replenishment of wardrobe and as to efficiency there is none. I must be doing or get off the earth like a noble Roman."[20]

Tilden visited Phelan in his office for a personal written plea: "I am doing nothing. The Government put an embargo on me physically, so I can't assist in the war. The country puts embargo on art so I can't model. That is a bit tough." The conversation was hastily concluded, on a scrap of paper, as Tilden hesitantly wrote: "I am separated from my wife and am now sans family, sans fortune, sans work. The Oakland investment was a wise one but there was no foreseeing the vagaries of a woman."[21]

Work as a Machinist

Some time during the fall of 1918 he obtained a job in a machine shop. However, he again appealed to Phelan, "to back me for the Fireman's statue. . . . I may be considered California's highest expression along a certain channel that is sculpture; and yet I am compelled to work in a machine shop to the disgrace of the state."[22] Ambivalent thoughts about this work surfaced in a *San Francisco Chronicle* news article a few months later. "When I was a boy," wrote Tilden, "I wanted to learn the machinist trade, but no shop would take me because of deafness. Odd to say, after more than thirty years I am taking up work I wanted to do long ago." The *Chronicle* acclaimed him as "the greatest living deaf-mute and the greatest sculptor west of the Rocky Mountains."[23]

Tilden's political interest had always been acute as a "profound thinker and student of affairs." With his Democratic party background, undoubtedly many were surprised to read on the front page of the morning newspaper—"Douglas Tilden Cast Vote For Harding." Quotes were printed from his letter to M. H. deYoung, editor of the paper: "From the first to the last I am against the idea of a league of nations as outlined by Wilson. De Tocqueville, a French author of much penetration, made the best analysis of the American democracy that has since been made by any writer, foreign or native, and he said that the only hope for the perpetuation of America as a republic is in a strict adhesion to form; that is, we are not to swerve an iota either to the right or the left from the spirit and letter of law as laid down in the constitution and buttressed by tradition."[24]

In the spring of 1921, Tilden's annoyance with his alma mater culminated in his organizing and spearheading the "Douglas Tilden Association for the Promotion of Art," to purchase, through membership fees, the famous *Bear Hunt* bronze statuary group from the California School for the Deaf. He hoped to build a pedestal and donate the monument to the state to be placed on the capital grounds in Sacramento.[25] Nothing came of this. "The purpose of the Association," wrote Tilden, "is to take art out of its present deplorable situation. . . . Our energy will be concentrated in the sincere belief that society cannot exist in its fullest vigor unless the importance of art as a constructive force in human progress continues to be recognized. Art makes a state wealthy by showing that life in it is worth while. Art enriches life itself."[26] Previously, June 28, 1916, the Board of Directors of the California School for the Deaf resolved to grant Tilden's request to regain possession of the *Bear Hunt* on payment of $679.40 (representing the Institution's interest in the statue).

The machine shop could not hold his creative energies. After a two-year silence in his correspondence file to Phelan, he again turns to his friend: "Can you grub stake me to a studio in San Francisco? It was erroneously reported in the press that I have a studio. I have none. . . . It is paralyzing, this machine shop. I am still a Hetch Hetchy dam full of unused potentials—hopelessly impotent because of lack of means for expression though always eager for an outlet . . . the things we have accomplished, seem to put on more and more importance with the lengthening time like the circles on a pond's surface. Your assistance to me personally has certainly been great."[27]

Tilden's marital problems did not improve and finally the *San Francisco Chronicle* headlined an article: "Mrs. Tilden Sued Artist for Divorce,—Wife Alleges Desertion in Complaint, Home Sold in Oakland," Mrs. Tilden disposed of the home and moved to San Francisco.[28]

Hollywood

The following year Tilden moved to Hollywood. He had obtained a well salaried position sculpturing extinct animals for historical and educational films.[29]

During the year, Tilden also modeled a bust of the actress Colleen Moore depicting her portrayal of the role of Salina Peake in the movie "So Big," and choosing her psychological interpretation of widowed old age. The model was to be cast in bronze[30] but no information seems obtainable regarding this work.

"I was nearly a year in Los Angeles," Tilden wrote later, assisting the First National Picture Company in the production of 'The Lost World' and the Hal Roach Company in making 'The Black Cyclone.' " It was interesting to get an insight of how those screen glories are created and, though my business was only toy making, I made a little money."[31]

When he returned to the Bay Area at Christmas, 1924, for a visit, his friends thought that he looked prosperous and happy. One friend greeted him: "I am glad you are a come back." "No," signed Tilden, "It's the world that's coming back to me."[32]

CHAPTER VII

BERKELEY AGAIN

A Final Farewell

1925-1935

"He has come back," wrote George West of the San Francisco *Call* in September, 1925. "Fresh complexioned, healthy, vigorous in mind and body. Tilden presents himself again as the master artist prepared once more to place his talents at the disposal of the community that already owes him so much."[1]

Tilden had saved enough money to purchase a small plot of land at 834 Channing Way, Berkeley. He eagerly wrote to the reporter: "I am building a small studio of rough boards with my own hands. I believe I was the first artist to have a studio in Berkeley and now after my wanderings I return to Berkeley, and am mooring my boat there for the last time."[2]

West was intrigued by and impressed with this California-born son of pioneers who, without speech and hearing, had become the foremost sculptor of the Pacific coast.

Tilden told West in this interview, conducted by written questions and answers, that he felt the capacity to create great works but "I am like war, useless unless there is a base of supply."[3]

As his crowning achievement he dreamed of a heroic statue on Telegraph Hill, he said, but refused to be specific about his ideas. "Sculptors are sometimes free with other's ideas," he told the reporter with a smile.[4]

Of modernists he thought little. "Cubists, modernists, etc.," he wrote in reply to West's question, "are fundamentalists and they do service by showing the importance of going to the root of things, but they stop there, and therefore their crudeness—which is not art."[5]

65

New Plans

On April 6, 1926, Tilden put the finishing touches on a clay model which he had envisioned for Telegraph Hill. He called it *The Bridge.* A reporter who came to take photographs and to interview Tilden said: "To most persons, the bridge proposed to connect San Francisco and Oakland is only a vague hope. To Tilden it is not a bridge. It is an idea." The reporter was intrigued by Tilden's use of the symbols of two figures kneeling in embrace across the waters of San Francisco Bay. "The girl represents the East bay—she is the personification of the meaning of home. The boy stands for productivity, wealth and fruitfulness of San Francisco. To the tenderness of the shy caress of the figures, Douglas Tilden has expressed the eagerness of youth in the male figure and a coyness about to yield in the maid."[6]

In November 1926, the honorary art society Delta Epsilon, invited Tilden to participate in an exhibition of etchings, sculpture, and lithographs by California artists to be held in Haviland Hall at the University of California. He exhibited his most recent sculpture, *Egypt,* a personification of the Universe, along with the *Bridge,* and an earlier sculpture showing San Francisco's recovery from the fire of 1906.[7]

Tilden continued his interest in the education of the deaf; in November he gave a talk on art to the honor society of the California School for the Deaf.[8] Tilden's interest in the administrative activities of the school remained strong—he became a watch dog. In the spring of 1927, he visited the legislature in Sacramento protesting a proposed relocation of the deaf from the Berkeley property.[9] Previous to this, he had been a strong force in the separation of the Blind and Deaf facilities in 1921.

The Row at the Legion of Honor

In the spring of 1929, the National Society of Sculpture held an exhibition at the California Palace of the Legion of Honor Museum in San Francisco. A controversy occurred between Phelan and Park Commissioner William F. Humphrey, when Tilden was not invited to participate. Finally Phelan wrote to Tilden that the committee was ready to receive Tilden's work and that he, Phelan, would pay the expense. Tilden was hurt. He answered, writing across the bottom of Phelan's letter, with a weak scribbling hand: "This is the first and only communication I have received from anybody connected with the exhibition, and I am not interested. If I had [been reimbursed for] expenses a year ago, I might now be ready with some worthy California art significance. I hope the exhibitors are happy. They can hear and speak. I hope, alas, all of you will be greater and better men for that reason."[10]

Saint Mary's College

During the fall of 1929 and the spring of 1930, Tilden went regularly to Saint Mary's College in Moraga, part-time, to guide a modeling class. Tilden had met Brother Cornelius, one of the revered professors of the College, in 1914, and their friendship had continued. Brother Cornelius saved the notes of the many conversations between him and Tilden when they had met. The professor thought these notes could be future dissertation material for students,[11] but they do not seem to have been preserved. Father Maurice Flynn, present Archivist of the school's Library, recalled that as a young man he had modeled his hands for Tilden whom he remembered as an outstanding person with "his smile always so ready." Saint Mary's College now has several models which Tilden gave to it: a small plaster model of *Junipero Serra*, a plaque of *St. John Baptist de la Salle,* a plaster medallion of *Junipero Serra* with praying hands, a Christ figure on a cross, and a massive plaster bust of *William Keith.*

The *Keith* bust was unveiled at the opening of the William Keith Gallery at the College on September 20, 1931. It was said that Tilden created the head in two days wholly from memory.[12] Keith's Jovian head is impressive, and it should be preserved in bronze before the plaster has completely crumbled.

On October 8, 1929, Tilden's long-time friend d'Estrella died. Tilden lost more than a friend: the men had been companions for sixty-four years. Tilden plucked a rose from his garden for his departed friend's lapel in the coffin and took leave from him in a Victorian eulogy in the *California News:* "Adieu, then, to the days of old, days of gold; adieu too, to Theophilus d'Estrella."[13]

Around Christmas, Tilden asked Phelan to "think of some way to keep me busy. I have a dozen magnificent licks still left in my system and my studio is full of sketches awaiting amplification." His dream of realizing this potential reached far and wide: "My plan would be to sail to Rome, finish the works there, exhibit first at the Paris Salon and then at Chicago, and finally dine opposite you at the Bohemian Club.[14]

In the spring of 1930, Tilden expressed his friendship for Phelan in the way Tilden knew best: "I have finished a life-sized model of what I think is your ideal hand of a woman and which I want to give to you as a token of old-time friendship and helpfulness."[15]

In April, Tilden's humor showing through his financial plight, appealed to Phelan: "I am in dire circumstances—so bad that the gas company has taken away the meters. Like Rabelais, I have to laugh to see an ordinary but useful company, which furnishes light to California, shut off the pipes from my perhaps useful studio, which furnishes light to America."[16] A few days later the lights and gas were miraculously restored. Tilden wrote Phelan of his appreciation and stated that he would "stump the state in sign language" if Phelan wanted to run again for political office.[17]

The clutches of the great financial depression gripped the land. Desperately, Tilden wrote to Phelan: "Should I apply for a state pension for aged people? . . . I do not know which way to turn."[18]

"It would seem that Mr. Tilden's friends in the East have the impression that he is a broken old man, thoroughly 'down and out'—an impression I would like to correct,"[19] wrote Wildey Meyers, a deaf man, in reply to an editorial in the *Deaf-Mutes' Journal*. "True, he is in reduced circumstances. But he is still an active, busy man. He still works with his clay from sheer love of his art, and does considerable reading and writing. And, he says he is still enjoying life immensely."[20]

Meyers and his family visited Tilden in his studio, and the children, age thirteen and eleven, marveled at this deaf man's ability to make cold clay and marble speak so eloquently. Meyers was impressed with what he felt was the essence of this man Tilden: "Mr. Tilden is a sturdy Western pioneer; as the greatest deaf sculptor the world has ever known, he shall be one of those—

> Whose distant footsteps echo
> Down the corridors of Time.[21]

California School for the Deaf

Tilden's interest in the children at the California School for the Deaf, brought him back to the classroom. In 1934 he informed one class about his early life as a student and about his work as a teacher and he "impressed upon the pupils the desirability of acquiring the reading habit in order to gain mastery of language."[22] Several young students visited his studio, and Sarah Boomer wrote about her excitement in seeing the statuary group of *The Bridge:* "It . . . shows two youthful figures stretched across a space, kissing. . . . Now that dream has come true and the bridge is being built."[23]

For a year and a half, Tilden worked on a prayer which he wanted delivered at the school's graduation. He wrote several letters to the superintendent, Elwood A. Stevenson, explaining that he wrote the prayer because, he felt it could tell the people more about the deaf by showing a deaf man's concern for the world, "in accordance with the Public Must Know Us dogma," which he fathered in the National Association of the Deaf earlier. The prayer ended: "Thy Kingdom Comes . . . for Thou art God, ever ancient and ever new and today the panoply of Goodness over our silent world where the sign language infuses Thy Grace into furthermost corners makes us free."[24] The prayer may have pleased his grandfather preacher, Adna A. Hecox.

Shortly after, Tilden's mother died. "Another page of California's early history was turned yesterday," noted the *San Francisco Examiner,* May 5, 1934, "with the passing of Mrs. Catherine Hecox Tilden Brown,"[25] who had crossed the plains in a covered wagon as a little girl; she had reached the age of ninety-three, active to the end with writing, sculpturing, and painting.

During the summer of 1934, Tilden, charged with new energies over the thoughts of a World's Fair on man-made Treasure Island in San Francisco Bay, enlarged the modeling room of his studio to twice its size. He needed more space to house the images of his concepts for a sculpture for the Golden Gate International Exposition.[26]

On September 23, Tilden was one of the hosts for a large party at "Villa Montalvo," at Saratoga, the country home of the late James D. Phelan. Phelan had willed his beautiful peninsula estate to the San Francisco Art Association of which Tilden was now an honorary member.[27]

In December, the *San Francisco Examiner* printed an illustrated article on Tilden, working over his latest masterpeice—the symbolic conception of San Francisco-Oakland Bay Bridge, which he said he had worked on for twenty years. The article noted: "Youth still guides the hand and rules the genius of 74-year-old Douglas Tilden, for years hailed at the West's greatest sculptor."[28]

In May 1935, the San Francisco Art Association Bulletin published excerpts from a letter they received from Tilden the month before: "I will be 75 on the first of May, I enclose my 'thinks' for the day which I faintly believe you may like. . . . Two simple laws: The first is: A work of Art which takes you at once to the great object that it wants to tell and does so without dragging you through barbs of harassing colors or confusing lines, is the only Art that is great. The second is: A work of Art which does not essay . . . to elevate you to Paradise is never, never great Art."[29]

Brother Cornelius accompanied Tilden, as his guest, to the annual alumni banquet of the San Francisco Art Institute held at Pierre's Chateau, May 1, 1935. There they celebrated his three-quarter-century birthday.[30]

It was his last. He enthusiastically continued to model on his new work. However, on July 31st, Tilden, feeling weak and lonely, sat down and wrote out his last will and testament bequeathing his bronze group The Bear Hunt "to my beloved Bohemian Club . . . worth fifty thousand dollars." This bequest hinged on the Bohemian Club paying off the indebtedness of the sculpture. The Club declined acceptance of the gift, and the mighty Bear Hunt still stands on the campus of the California School for the Deaf—cherished through the years by hundreds of students. Tilden also bequeathed to the Bohemian Club a portrait of himself painted in 1895 by "the elder Partington."[31] He willed everything else to his daughter Gladys; his son Willoughby, an invalid, had died several years before.

Six days later, on the morning of August 6th, an old friend and chess-player crony, Leandro Maldonado, called on Tilden. Maldonado pushed open the door of Tilden's studio and found him, lying face down on the floor. He lay within reach of his tools in front of his most recent, yet unfinished, clay model—a frieze for one of the Golden Gate Exposition Buildings on Treasure Island. The gas flame was still burning under the scorched empty pan on the stove. Tilden, the first great sculptor of the West had been dead for two days.[32] A heart attack felled him as he was doing, to the last, the work he loved.

Funeral arrangements were made by the stricken Bessie who had remained his loyal friend despite their divorce. The Reverend George Goertner, delivered the silent eulogy at the Mountain View Cemetery Crematorium in Oakland.[33]

Douglas Tilden, the deaf genius, devoted his life to his art and to creating a better understanding between the two worlds of the hearing and the deaf. He worked for his credo that art can transcend our diversities and unite us all, and he left a visual heritage in bronze as a testimony of that turbulent and magnificent era at the turn of the century in California.

NOTES

CHAPTER I

[1]*The National Cyclopedia of American Biography* (Clifton, New Jersey: James T. White & Co.), p. 489.

[2]Marie Valhasky, "The Story of Margaret M. Hecox," *Overland Monthly,* XIX (May 1892), 535.

[3]"Noted Sculptor reveals New Incident of Early Pioneers." This is a two-column newspaper article found in a clipping file in the California Room, Oakland Public Library. Across the top it says "Berkeley, Gazette, 5/15/68," but the date is incorrect; I have not been able to locate the original article.

[4]Marie Valhasky, "The Story of Margaret M. Hecox" (second part), *Overland Monthly,* XX (July 1892), 98.

[5]Charles Volney Anthony, *Fifty Years of Methodism* (San Francisco: Methodist Book Concern Co., 1901), p. 7.

[6]Valhasky, *op. cit.,* July 1892, p. 98.

[7]*Ibid.*

[8]*Ibid.*

[9]Hubert Howe Bancroft, *History of California* (San Francisco: A. L. Bancroft & Co., 1885), III, 780.

[10]Valhasky, *op. cit.,* July 1892, p. 98.

[11]Santa Cruz Museum folder, "A Brief History of the Santa Cruz Museum," 6 panels (n.d.).

[12]Caroline H. Burnes and Catherine M. Ramger, A History of the *California School for the Deaf,* 1860–1960 (Berkeley: 1960), p. 118, printed by the Students, California School for the Deaf, Berkeley, California, January, 1960.

[13]Charles Smith, "This Sketch of Douglas Tilden from an Old Book," *Silent Worker,* XVI:3 (December 1903), 35.

[14]Burnes and Ramger, *op. cit.,* p. 118.

[15]J. Warring Wilkinson, "Our Art Possibilities," *Overland Monthly,* II (March 1869), pp. 248–254.

[16]J. Warring Wilkinson, papers, Bancroft, c. 1891.

[17]Communication, January 11, 1915, to Board of Directors, California School for the Deaf, from Douglas Tilden, Carbon copy, typed.

[18]"Douglas Tilden," *Silent Worker,* VII:2 (October 1894), p. 1.

[19]*Ibid.*

[20]*Ibid.*

[21]Original hand-written minutes of the meetings of the Excelsior Debating Society, California School for the Deaf, 1871–1876, Archives, California School for the Deaf, Berkeley.

[22]J. Warring Wilkinson, papers, Bancroft Library.

[23]Douglas Tilden, "Deaf-Mutes and their Education," *Overland Monthly,* V (May 1885), PP. 504–510.

[24]Douglas Tilden, "A Forgotten Page of an Institution History," *American Annals of the Deaf,* XXXII, No. 1 (1887), pp. 11–16.

[25]Douglas Tilden, "Articulation in a New Light," *American Annals of the Deaf,* XXXII, No. 2 (1887), p. 98.

[26]Douglas Tilden, "Signs and Words,"*American Annals of the Deaf,* XXXII, No. 3 (1887), p. 176.

[27]Douglas Tilden, "The Artist's Testament," *Overland Monthly,* April 1888, pp. 395–402. (written under pseudonym Clarence Stairly).

[28]Kevin Starr, *Americans and the California Dream,* 1850–1915, (New York: Oxford University Press, 1973), p. 173.

[29]Communication, January 11, 1915, *op. cit.*

[30]William A. Caldwell, *The California News,* March 23, 1895.

[31]Theophilus d'Estrella, "Illustrated History of Big Tree Camp: Aug. 16th to Sept. 9th, 1882," original hand-written journal, Archives, California School for the Deaf, Berkeley.

[32]"Douglas Tilden," *op. cit.*

[33]*Ibid.*

[34]*Ibid.*

[35]Excerpts from Minutes of the meeting of June, 1887, of the Board of Directors, of the California School for the Deaf (carbon copy, typed), p. 50.

[36]"Douglas Tilden," *op. cit.*

CHAPTER II

[1]Editorial, *The Weekly News* (of the Institution for the Deaf and Dumb, and the Blind, now the California School for the Deaf), Berkeley, September 17, 1887, p. 2.

[2]*Ibid.,* September 10, 1887.

[3]*Ibid.*, October 1, 1887.

[4]Douglas Tilden, "School for the Improved Instruction of the Deaf," *The Weekly News,* October 15, 1887.

[5]Editorial, *The Weekly News,* November 19, 1887.

[6]*Ibid.*, April 14, 1888.

[7]Communication, January 11, 1915, to Board of Directors, California School for the Deaf, from Douglas Tilden. Carbon copy, typed.

[8]Editorial, *The Weekly News,* May 19, 1888.

[9]Communication, *op. cit.*

[10]*Ibid.*

[11]Editorial, *The Weekly News,* September 8, 1888.

[12]*Ibid.*

[13]*Ibid.*, December 22, 1888.

[14]Communication, *op. cit.*

[15]*Ibid.*

[16]*Ibid.*

[17]Douglas Tilden, "How the French Enjoy Life," *The Weekly News,* March 16, 1889 (reprinted from *The Deaf-Mutes' Journal,* New York).

[18]Douglas Tilden, "Paris," *The Weekly News,* January 12, 1889 (reprinted from *The Deaf-Mutes' Journal.* December 27, 1888).

[19]T. H. d'Estrella, "A Summer Trip to Paris," *The Weekly News,* February 15, 1890, p. 3.

[20]Douglas Tilden, "Oignons Sautes." *The Weekly News,* March 15, 1890. pp. 2, 3.

[21]"Tilden's New York," *The Weekly News,* April 19, 1890 (reprinted from *The Deaf-Mutes' Journal,* New York).

[22]Editorial, *The Weekly News,* June 7, 1890.

[23]D'Estrella, "The Itemizer," *The Weekly News,* November 15, 1890. Mr. d'Estrella wrote the Itemizer column for more than forty-five years for the weekly then monthly newspaper for the California School for the Deaf. He was the school's first pupil, and a life long personal friend of Douglas Tilden, receiving many letters from him, excerpts of which appeared frequently in his column.

[24] "Great Artists," *San Francisco Bulletin,* February 28, 1891. Editorial, "Art in San Francisco," *San Francisco Bulletin,* March 14, 1891.

[25]"The Little Acrobat—Dogulas Tilden's Latest Sculpture," unidentified newspaper clipping from an old scrapbook from the Hecox family, Santa Cruz Public Library.

[26]*San Francisco Examiner,* January 1, 1893 and January 3, 1893.

[27]"A Letter From Tilden," *The Weekly News,* September 12, 1891.

[28]Parisina, "The Silent Sculptor," *Argonaut* (Paris: June 8, 1892).

[29]*Ibid.*

[30]Communication, *op. cit.*

[31]"Correspondence from Europe—From Tilden," *The Weekly News,* September 26, 1891.

[32]Communication, *op. cit.*

[33]Joaquin Miller, *The San Francisco Call,* October 16, 1892.

[34]Henry Meade Bland, "Two Representative Men of California, Benjamin Ide Wheeler and Douglas Tilden," *Overland Monthly,* November 1906, p. 329.

[35]"Douglas Tilden," *The Silent Worker,* Trenton, New Jersey, October, 1894, Vol. VII, 2, pp. 1–4.

[36]*Ibid.*

[37]Rossiter Johnson, ed., *The History of the World Columbian Exposition* (New York: D. Appleton, 1897, 1898), III, 409.

[38]Communication, *op. cit.*

[39]*Ibid.*

[40]D'Estrellla, "The Itemizer," The Weekly News, March 10, 1894.

[41]*Ibid.,* date not known.

CHAPTER III

[1]Richard D. Mandel, *Paris 1900: the great World's Fair* (Toronto: University of Toronto Press, 1967), p. 71.

[2]William Harlan Hale and the editors, *The World of Rodin* (New York: Time-Life Books), p. 79.

[3]Bruce Porter, *Art in California,* 1916.

[4]*Catalogue of the Mark Hopkins Institute of Art,* 1901.

[5]"The Deaf Sculptor's New Class at the Hopkins Institute," *San Francisco Call,* October 26, 1894.

[6]*Ibid.*

[7]"Works of Art," *Weekly News,* December 1, 1894, p. 7.

[8]*San Francisco Call,* October 26, 1894.

[9]*Ibid.,* February 25, 1895, p. 10.

[10]D'Estrella, "The Itemizer," October 27, 1894.

[11]"Who Got the Durham Fund," The *Examiner, San Francisco,* April 8, 1895, p. 4.

[12]Dorothy Kaucher, *James Duval Phelan* (Saratoga: Gallery Committee of the Montalvo Association, 1965), p. 11.

[13]D'Estrella, "The Itemizer," *Weekly News,* February 16, 1895.

[14]*San Francisco Chronicle*, December 20, 1895.

[15]Newspaper article, n.d., pasted in an old scrapbook at the Santa Cruz Public Library.

[16]D'Estrella, "The Itemizer," *The California News* (formerly the *Weekly News*), March 6, 1897.

[17]*San Francisco Chronicle*, September 6, 1897, p. 8.

[18]William Dallam Armes, "Douglas Tilden," *Overland Monthly*, February 1898, p. 149.

[19]Editorial, *Overland Monthly*, March 1898.

[20]Armes, *op. cit.*, p. 144.

[21]*Ibid.*

[22]Loredo Taft, *The History of American Sculpture* (New York, London: MacMillan Co., 1903), p. 536.

[23]Armes, *op. cit.*, 1898, p. 153.

[24]Robert and Carol Sibley, *California Pilgrimage* (Berkeley, Calif.: printed by Lederer, Street and Zeus, 1952), p. 161.

[25]"Greater University is Inaugurated," *Berkeley Daily Gazette*, May 12, 1900.

[26]D'Estrella, "The Itemizer," *The California News*, January 5, 1901.

[27]W. W. Robinson, "The Strange Case of Thomas Valentine," *Westways, March, 1946, pp. 32, 33.*

[28]*Ibid.*

[29]D'Estrella, "The Itemizer," *The California News*, January 6, 1900.

[30]Communication, January 11, 1915, to Board of Directors, California School for the Deaf, from Douglas Tilden, Carbon copy. Typed.

[31]D'Estrella, *The California News*, January 6, 1900.

CHAPTER IV

[1]D'Estrella, "The Itemizer," *The California News*, Berkeley, April 6, 1901.

[2]Brother Cornelius, *Keith, Old Master of California* (Fresno: Academy Library Guild, 1957), II, 293.

[3]D'Estrella, "The Itemizer, October 26, 1901.

[4]*Ibid.*, May 3, 1902.

[5]"The Sculpture of Douglas Tilden," *Silent Worker*, XVI:3 (December 1903), 33–41, 44.

[6]*Ibid.*

[7]D'Estrella, "The Itemizer," May 3, 1902.

[8]*Ibid.*

[9]*Ibid.*, May 30, 1903 (reprinted from *Deaf-Mutes' Journal*).

[10]"Arrival of President Roosevelt," *San Francisco Chronicle*, May 14, 1903, pp. 2, 7.

[11]*Ibid.*, illustration.

[12]Letter from Betty Monkman, Registrar, Office of the Curator, The White House, Washington, June 4, 1975.

[13]Letter from James L. Brown, Park Manager, U.S. Department of Interior, National Park Service, Sagamore Hill Historic Site, Cove Neck Road, Box 304, Oyster Bay, New York 11771, July 3, 1975.

[14]Joseph Henry Jackson, editor, *The Western Gate* (New York: Farrar, Straus & Young, 1952), pp. 263–264.

[15]D'Estrella, "The Itemizer," February 7, 1903, p. 5.

[16]Chicago *Record Herald*, June 30, 1907.

[17]*Ibid.*

[18]*Ibid.*

[19]"Memorial Statue Stands Unveiled," *The Morning Oregonian*, Portland, Oregon, May 31, 1906, p. 10.

[20]D'Estrella, "The Itemizer," May 9, 1903.

[21]D'Estrella, "The Itemizer, January 16, 1904, p. 5 (reprinted from the Christmas number of the Mark Hopkins Institute's *Review of Art*, San Francisco), 1903.

[22]D'Estrella, "The Itemizer," September 9, 1905.

[23]Eric Howard, "Stephen M. White," in Rockwell D. Hunt, ed., *California and Californians* (Chicago: Lewis Publishing Company, 1926), III, 129.

[24]Editorial, *The California News*, October 28, 1905 (copied from the *Los Angeles Times*).

[25]*Ibid.*

[26]"Deaf Mute Sculptor Wins Fame" (from an old scrapbook, at the California School for the Deaf), *Chicago Record Herald*, June 30, 1907.

[27]Douglas Tilden, "Zenoisms," *Deaf-Mutes' Journal*, New York, February 23, 1905.

[28]*Ibid.*

[29]Unsigned manuscript in Tilden's handwriting, Library, California School for the Deaf, circa 1900–1905.

[30]D'Estrella, "The Itemizer," November 15, 1902.

[31]*Ibid.*

[32]Douglas Tilden, "Deaf-Mutes and the World of Pantomime," *San Francisco Call*, March 30, 1903, p. 7.

[33]D'Estrella, "The Itemizer," October 28, 1905, p. 5.

[34]*Ibid.*, January 20, 1906.

[35]D'Estrella, "The Itemizer,"—"California Association of the Deaf," January 5, 1907, p. 3.

[36]Douglas Tilden, "The New and Noble Order of Americans," *Deaf-Mutes' Journal,* New York, October 5, 1905.

[37]D'Estrella, "The Itemizer," March 3, 1906.

CHAPTER V

[1]Letter, dated May 10, 1906, from Douglas Tilden to Mr. Dusuzeau, Paris, France. Printed in *Le Journal des Sourds-Muets, Paris* (in French).

[2]*Ibid.*

[3]Letter, April 26, 1906, from Douglas Tilden to James D. Phelan, Phelan papers, Bancroft Library, Berkeley.

[4]*San Francisco Chronicle,* August 13, 1906, p. 1.

[5]*Ibid.*

[6]Letter, August 14, 1906, from Tilden to Phelan, Phelan papers, Bancroft Library.

[7]D'Estrella, "The Itemizer," *The California News,* September 15, 1906.

[8]Letter, October 14, 1906, Tilden to Phelan, Phelan papers, Bancroft Library.

[9]D'Estrella, "The Itemizer," *The California News,* May 25, 1907.

[10]"Deaf-Mute Sculptor Wins Fame," June 30, 1907, Chicago *Record-Herald.*

[11]*San Francisco Chronicle,* November 18, 1907, p. 1.

[12]Letter, January 26, 1907, Tilden to Phelan, Phelan papers, Bancroft Library.

[13]D'Estrella, "The Itemizer," *The California News,* March 9, 1907, p. 5.

[14]"Laurels of Great Love Placed On Beautiful White memorial," Los Angeles, *Daily Times,* Section II, p. 1, December 12, 1908.

[15]James M. Goode, *The Outdoor Sculpture of Washington, D.C.* (The Smithsonian Institution Press, Publication 4829), 1974, p. 25.

[16]Los Angeles *Daily Times, op cit.*

[17]Los Angeles *Daily Times,* editorial, December 11, 1908, p. 4.

[18]Los Angeles *Daily Times, op cit.,* December 12, 1908.

[19]*Ibid.*

[20]Los Angeles *Times,* July 15, 1958.

[21]Oakland *Tribune,* September 18, 1911, Second Section, p. 1.

[22]*Ibid.*

[23]*Ibid.*

[24]D'Estrella, "The Itemizer," *The California News,* December 1912.

[25]*Ibid.,* April 1913.

[26]*Ibid.*

[27]*Ibid.*

[28]Printed material from old Bohemian Club records.

[29]D'Estrella, "The Itemizer," *The California News,* November 15, 1914.

[30]Letter, December 6, 1914, Tilden to Phelan, Phelan papers, Bancroft Library.

[31]San Francisco *Bulletin,* July 17, 1914, p. 4.

[32]Letter, January 23, 1915, Tilden to Phelan, Phelan papers, Bancroft Library.

CHAPTER VI

[1]Wayne Craven, *Sculpture in America* (New York: Crowell, 1968), p. 420.

[2]*Ibid.*

[3]*Ibid.*

[4]Patricia Janis Broder, *Bronzes of the American West* (New York: Harry N. Abrams, Inc., 1975), p. 18.

[5]Kevin Starr, *Americans and the California Dream, 1850–1915,* (New York: Oxford University Press, 1973), p. 286.

[6]Letter, October 25, 1915, from Tilden to Phelan, Phelan Papers, Bancroft Library, University of California, Berkeley.

[7]Letter, February 23, 1916, from Tilden to Ella S. Mighels, Bancroft, Berkeley.

[8]Ibid.

[9]Letter, June 11, 1917, from Tilden to Laurance E. Milligan, Archives, California School for the Deaf, Berkeley.

[10]Douglas Tilden, "Value of Art to the Deaf," *Proceedings of the Convention of the American Instructors of the Deaf,* Hartford Connecticut (June 29—July 3, 1917). pp. 85–90.

[11]*Ibid.*

[12]*Ibid.*

[13]*Ibid.*

[14]*Ibid.*

[15]*Ibid.*

[16]Letter, February 17, 1918, from Tilden to Milligan, Archives, California School for the Deaf.

[17]Letter, May 19, 1918, from Tilden to Phelan, Phelan Papers, Bancroft Library, Berkeley.

[18]Letter, January 20, 1919, from Tilden to Milligan, Archives, California School for the Deaf.

[19]Letter, August 10, 1919, from Tilden to Phelan, Phelan Papers, Bancroft Library, Berkeley.

[20]Letter, August 15, 1919, from Tilden to Phelan, Phelan Papers, Bancroft Library, Berkeley.

[21]Handwritten notes, n.d., from Tilden to Phelan, Phelan Papers, Bancroft Library, Berkeley.

[22]Letter, October 17, 1919, from Tilden to Phelan, Phelan Papers, Bancroft Library, Berkeley.

[23]"Douglas Tilden Gives up Art to be Machinist," *San Francisco Chronicle*, January 12, 1920, p. 1.

[24]"Douglas Tilden to Cast Vote for Harding," *San Francisco Chronicle*, October 31, 1920, Second Section, col. 5.

[25]D'Estrella, "Itemizer," *The California News*, March 1921.

[26]*Printed statement of purpose*, n.d.

[27]Letter, October 22, 1923, from Tilden to Phelan, Phelan Papers, Bancroft Library.

[28]"Mrs. Tilden Sues Artist for Divorce," *San Francisco Chronicle*, April 23, 1925, p. 13.

[29]Editorial, *The California News*, September 1924, p. 11.

[30]*Ibid.*, January 1925, pp. 65–66.

[31]"Noted Artist Rises Anew After 20 Years," *The San Francisco Call*, September 12, 1925, p. 20.

[32]Editorial, *The California News*, January 1925, pp. 65–66.

CHAPTER VII

[1]George West, "Noted Artist Rises Anew After 20 Years," San Francisco *Call*, September 12, 1925.

[2]*Ibid.*

[3]*Ibid.*

[4]*Ibid.*

[5]*Ibid.*

[6]*San Francisco Chronicle*, April 7, 1926.

[7]D'Estrella, "The Itemizer," *The California News*, December 1926.

[8]Winfield S. Runde, "Here and There," *The California News*, November 1926.

[9]Letter, Tilden to Phelan, Phelan papers, March 17, 1927, Bancroft Library.

[10]*Ibid.*, April 17, 1929.

[11]"The Greatest and Noblest Genius Among our Western Sculptors," *St. Mary's Collegian,* Moraga, September 30, 1935.

[12]"Sculptor Honors Painter," *San Francisco Chronicle,* September 10, 1931.

[13]Douglas Tilden, "California and Theophilus d'Estrella, *The California News,* November 7, 1929.

[14]Letter, Tilden to Phelan, Phelan papers, December 17, 1929, Bancroft Library.

[15]*Ibid.,* March 30, 1930.

[16]*Ibid.,* April 15, 1930.

[17]*Ibid.,* April 22, 1930.

[18]*Ibid.,* June 22, 1930.

[19]Wildey Meyers, "Douglas Tilden," The *Deaf-Mutes' Journal,* New York, March 19, 1931.

[20]*Ibid.,*

[21]*Ibid.*

[22]"The Deaf in General," *The California News,* January 25, 1934.

[23]Sarah Boomer, "Work of Douglas Tilden," *The California News* (Pupils' Edition), April 12, 1934.

[24]Letter, Tilden to Elwood Stevenson, March 11, 1934, enclosure.

[25]San Francisco *Examiner,* May 5, 1934.

[26]Runde, *op. cit.,* September 25, 1934.

[27]*The California News,* October 1934.

[28]San Francisco *Examiner,* December (undetermined day), 1934, copied in *The California News,* February 25, 1935.

[29]Letter, Tilden to San Francisco Art Association *Bulletin,* May 1935, Vol. II, No. 1.

[30]*St. Mary's Collegian,* September 1935.

[31]Documents, Alameda County Courthouse, Oakland, California.

[32]San Francisco *Examiner,* August 7, 1935.

[33]Oakland *Tribune,* August 7, 1935. Other obituaries: "Death Ends a Notable Career," San Francisco *Call-Bulletin,* August 6, 1935; "Sculptor Dies in Studio," *San Francisco Chronicle,* August 7, 1935; "Douglas Tilden, 75, Sculptor, is Dead," New York *Times,* August 8, 1935.

CHRONOLOGY: DOUGLAS TILDEN

(1860–1935).

1860	Born May 1, in Chico, California, to Dr. William Peregrine Tilden, M.D. and Catherine Hecox Tilden.
1861	Moved to Stockton where Dr. Tilden became the resident physician of what is now the Stockton State Hospital.
1864 or 1865	Lost hearing and speech from scarlet fever during an epidemic in Stockton.
1866	January 25, entered the California Institution for the Education and Care of the Indigent Deaf and Dumb, and the Blind, San Francisco. Now called the California School for the Deaf, Berkeley.
1867	Attended the laying of the cornerstone for a new school building in Berkeley, September 26, 1867.
1869	California School for the Deaf relocated at permanant site in Berkeley.
1870	Grandfather Adna A. Hecox, cabinet maker and lighthouse keeper, taught Douglas carpentry during vacations and weekends at his home in Santa Cruz.
1873	His father, Dr. W. P. Tilden, died in May.
1879	Graduated from the California School for the Deaf. Passed entrance exams for the University of California, Berkeley, registered, but decided to accept a position as teacher at the California School for the Deaf. He held this position for eight years.
1881	Took vacation backpacking trip to Yosemite where he ascended Half Dome by rope.
1882	Studied drawing and painting with Virgil Williams at the San Francisco Art Association's School of Design for one month during

summer vacation. Continued drawing during the year and worked on perfecting a rotary engine.

Went camping and sketching for two weeks with life-long friend Theophilus Hope d'Estrella to Duncan Mills, Russian River.

1883 Became interested in sculpture. Studied for one month with Marion Wells (leading sculptor in San Francisco.) In the fall, purchased a barrel of clay, took possession of an abandoned laundry building on the school grounds, and worked alone in his spare time at sculpture modeling for the next four years.

1885 Wrote "Deaf Mutes and their Education," published in the West's leading magazine *The Overland Monthly*.

Modeled a small statuette, the *Tired Wrestler*. When this came to the attention of the school board, they offered him the opportunity to study in New York and Paris with proceeds from the Durham Fund—$500 per year (1887).

Finished medallion bas-relief head of *Poetry*.

1886 Studied Dante's Divine Comedy and Inferno with illustrations by Gustave Dore. Made bas-relief based on these studies.

1887 Resigned teaching position in June. Spent the summer at the Santa Cruz lighthouse where his aunt was now the keeper. Helped collect shells for what later became the nucleus of the Santa Cruz City Museum.

Left Berkeley, September 12, arrived in New York six days later. Studied at the National Academy of Fine Arts under Ward during the day, and in the evening at the Gotham Student's League under Flagg and Mowbray for eight months.

1888 Arrived in Paris, end of May, and rented a studio at #1 Rue de Clerc. Began work on the *National Game* (later known as *The Baseball Player*.) Worked privately for five months under the guidance of deaf sculptor Paul Chopin—medalist in the Paris Salon.

1889 *The Baseball Player*, plaster, was accepted in the Salon. Attended Buffalo Bill Cody's Wild West Show in Paris on July 4 with his visiting friend Theophilus Hope d'Estrella.

Assisted in inaugurating the first International Congress of the Deaf, held July 11–17 during the Paris Universal Exposition, acting as vice-president.

1890   *The Baseball Player,* now cast in bronze, was accepted at the Salon. Shipped to the United States August 5.

The Tired Boxer, plaster, was accepted in the Salon and received an Honorable Mention.

Attended the Twelfth Annual Convention of Instructors of the Deaf and the First International Convention in America in New York, August 23–29, returning immediately to Paris.

Studied with animal sculptor Emmanuel Fremiet at the Jardin des Plantes during the winter and spring, (1890–91).

1891   The bronze *Baseball Player* was exhibited as the only American-artist entry in the Art Loan Exhibition at George C. Shreve and Co.'s Art Room, San Francisco.

The Baseball Player was unveiled July 8 in Golden Gate Park, San Francisco. Purchased as a gift to the city by Mr. W. E. Brown commemorating the talent of Douglas Tilden.

The Tired Boxer, bronze cast, was accepted in the Salon.

Prepared paper, "Higher Education of the Deaf," for the British Congress of the Deaf held in Glasgow, Scotland, August 3.

Moved to a larger studio, #14 Rue du Moulin de Beurre. Began work on the *Bear Hunt* in August.

Published ten "Half-Hour Lessons for the Deaf" in *The Educator.*

1892   Exhibited the *Bear Hunt,* bronze cast, in the Salon. Was appointed European member of the jury for sculpture for the World's Columbian Exposition to be held in Chicago in 1893.

Young Acrobat, bronze, marble, and gilt, exhibited in the Salon.

The Tired Boxer was purchased by subscription of prominent men and installed in the new Olympic Club Building in San Francisco, January 2, 1893.

Published "Art, and What California Should Do About Her" in the *Overland Monthly,* May 1892.

1893   Financial panic and depression.

Exhibited four peices at the World's Columbian Exposition in Chicago: the plaster *Baseball Player,* the plaster *Tired Boxer,* the bronze and marble *Young Acrobat,* and the bronze *Bear Hunt.*

Prepared paper for the World's Congress for the Deaf, Chicago, "Art Education of the Deaf."

Another deaf friend, Granville Seymour Redmond, arrived November 25, in Paris to study painting—stayed with Tilden.

1894   Exhibited plaster *Football Players* in Salon.

Because of financial conditions, sailed from Paris June 13, via New York, arrived in San Francisco in July in time to get a glimpse of the Mid-Winter Exposition in Golden Gate Park.

Set up studio in abandoned Virgil William's studio in the old Art Gallery at Woodward Gardens, 14 and Jessie Streets, San Francisco.

Accepted position to found the first department of modeling at the Mark Hopkins Institute of Art, a position he held for seven years. Classes began October 29.

Was elected member of the Bohemian Club December 5.

1895   The bronze *Bear Hunt* arrived at the California School for the Deaf February 28.

Received first commission from Mayor James D. Phelan of San Francisco to create the *Admission Day* monument (also known as *Phelan's Monument* or *Native Sons*).

Was voted Honorary member of Bohemian Club.

Bronze *Bear Hunt* exhibited for several months at the Mark Hopkins Institute of Art.

1896   Married Elizabeth Delano Cole, also deaf, June 6, in her Oakland home. Willis Polk, architect, acted as best man.

1897   *Admission Day* monument unveiled September 5 at Market, Turk, and Mason streets, San Francisco.

Received commission to create the Peter Donohue Memorial Monument (*The Mechanics*).

Received commission from Mayor Phelan for a statue of Vasco Nunez de Balboa for Golden Gate Park. (Never realized because of the Spanish-American War.)

1898   Was awarded first prize for the best short story for The *Overland Monthly* magazine. "The Poverty of Fortune," March 1898.

Exhibited bronze *Football Players* at the Spring Exhibition at the Mark Hopkins Institute of Art. Mayor Phelan awarded this to the winner of two out of three football games between Stanford University and the University of California. California won.

Accepted appointment to the Mayor's committeee for adornment of the city. Sometime in the late nineties Tilden created a marble bust of *Father John Young* of the University of Santa Clara and also the bronze *Valentine* memorial monument.

1900   Daughter Gladys born January 5.

White plaster *Football Players* exhibited in Paris Universelle Exposition receiving a "Medaille de Bronze."

Accepted appointment as Professor of Sculpture by the Regents of the University of California. (The Mark Hopkins Institute of Art was an affiliated college of the University at that time.)

Exhibited four pieces at the Mark Hopkins Institute of Art Exhibition.

Attended the unveiling of the *Football Players,* May 12, at the University of California, Berkeley, campus.

1901   Resigned as Professor of Sculpture in June to set up his own studio in the carriage house of his Victorian residence at 1545 Webster, Oakland.

Exhibited four pieces at the Mark Hopkins Institute of Art Exhibition.

Attended the unveiling of *The Mechanics,* May 15, at Market, Bush, and Battery streets, San Francisco.

Exhibited the plaster *Football Players* at the Pan American Exposition, Buffalo, New York.

1902   Submitted plaster model, 9' high by 7 ½' × 11' base, for *Ulysses S. Grant* memorial monument competition in Washington, D.C. (Not Accepted.)

1903   Received commission in a national competition for the *California Volunteers* (Memorial to the Spanish-American War volunteer infantrymen.)

Was elected Royal Fellow of the Society of Arts in London.

Submitted model for *Oregon Volunteers.*

Received offer to create architectural decoration for the St. Louis Louisianna Purchase Exposition.

Son Willoughby born September 16.

Submitted model for the McKinley Memorial statue in Philadelphia. (Not accepted.)

1904   Received commission for the *Oregon Volunteers* for Portland, Oregon. Received Commemorative Gold Medal for the architectural decoration over the south entrance of the varied Industries Building at the St. Louis Exposition.

1905   Finished the *Joseph Le Conte* Memorial tablet for the Yosemite Lodge. Spearheaded organizing the California Association of the Deaf.

Oregon Volunteers finished.
California Volunteers in process.

1906   Left for Portland, Oregon April 14.
Devastating earthquake and fire in Bay Area, April 18. Tilden still in Oregon. Studio in Oakland slightly damaged; house damaged more. The finished plaster model of *Father Junipero Serra* survived intact as did the *Stephen White* memorial model. In San Francisco, the *Mechanics* and *Admission Day* survived intact; the *Tired Boxer* was destroyed.
California Volunteers unveiled August 12. (This statue was in Chicago being cast into bronze at the time of the disaster.)

1907   *U.S. Senator Stephen M. White* statue completed.
Visited Chicago to check casting of *Junipero Serra*. Attended the National Association of the Deaf Convention in Jamestown.
Modeled statuette *Golden Gate*. Later gave this plaster as a gift to Mr. and Mrs. Jack London, November 12, 1916. Bronze cast made in 1969. Now in The Oakland Museum Collection.
Junipero Serra monument unveiled November 17 in Golden Gate Park, San Francisco.

1908   *Stephen M. White* memorial monument unveiled December 11 in Los Angeles.

1909   Received Gold Medal award for the plaster medallion of *Father Junipero Serra* at the Alaska-Yukon-Pacific Exposition, Seattle, Washington. This same image was designed for the granite cross which stands at Monterey, California commemorating the spot where Serra landed in 1770 (Historic Landmark #128).

1910   Started work on *Twelve Stages of Man* represented by twelve bronze bas-relief placques for the McElroy Fountain in Lakeside Park, Oakland.
Was elected president of the California Association of the Deaf.

1911   Delegate of American Society of Deaf Artists to American Federation of Arts, Washington, D.C. (by correspondence).

1912   Exhibited the *Twelve Stages of Man* plaster casts and a plaster bas-relief medallion of *Father Junipero Serra* at the Annual Exhibition of the members of the Bohemian Club.
Bronze bas-reliefs placed on the fountain July 6, 1912.

1913	Created a fabricated figure for the Bohemian Club Grove play *"The Fall of Ug."* Worked on clay sketch of *General Bidwell* for Chico. (Not used.)
1914	Worked on model, *Modern Civilization,* for the Pan Pacific Exposition to be held in San Francisco in 1915. (Not used.) Was honored as foremost sculptor in California in a stained-glass window—one of thirteen windows honoring artists in Hall of Fame in Native Sons Auditorium.
1915–1916	Wrote novel, "The Dummy," later renamed "The Gap," Unpublished as far as is known.
1917	Wrote "The Value of Art to the Deaf" for the Program of the Twenty-First Convention of American Instructors of the Deaf, Hartford, Connecticut.
1918	Moved out of his studio to 314 Hobart, Oakland.
1920	Became a machinist.
1921	Organized The Douglas Tilden Association for Promotion of Arts.
1924	Moved to Hollywood to work in Hal Roach Studio making fabricated animals for movie sets. Modeled bust of actress Colleen Moore from movie "So Big" (whereabouts unknown). Wife filed suit for divorce. Built a studio at 834 Channing Way, Berkeley. Exhibited three small works with California artists in Haviland Hall, at the University of California.
1926	Exhibited small works in the Annual Winter Exhibition of the Bohemian Club. Finished work on *The Bridge.* Divorce final. Worked full time in studio.
1929–1930	Assisted Brother Cornelius in the Art Department at Saint Mary's College, Moraga, California.
1931	Created plaster bust of painter *William Keith* for the opening of the Keith Gallery at Saint Mary's College.
1932	Donated sculptured hand (or plaster model) to be included in the contents of the cornerstone box for the new Educational Building of the California School for the Deaf, Berkeley.

Architectural decorations exhibited in the Bohemian Club Annual held February 13-27.

Joined Commonwealth Club; interested in City Planning section.

1934   His mother, author and sculptress Catherine Hecox Tilden Brown, died.

1935   Listed in S. F. Museum's catalogue for the exhibit "Thirty Years of California Sculpture," August 16-October 20. (Not known whether work was displayed.)

Found dead in his studio, August 6.

THE UNVEILING OF THE FOUNTAIN

by Mrs. Laura Redden Searing
(deaf poetess)

This delicate shaft, so slender, yet so strong
   How proudly it upbears
Its graceful burden, perfect as a song,
   The which it crown-like wears!

Meet art thou, O, fair figure, to hold up
   With arms untired and young,
Th' unwritten book; like to an unfilled cup,
   Like to a song unsung.

That splendid Future, toward which thy face
   With such glad pride is turned,
Shall grasp and hold thee on a long embrace
   Till all its fame is earned.

They chronicle, as yet unwrit, is all
   That older hands have won;
And't will be gladly more, whate'er befall
   Beneath the onlooking sun.

For it shall be the joy of him who stands
   All rugged at thy feet
To bear aloft the flag within his hands
   Each nook of earth to greet.

Ah, fountain! let they virginal waters gush
   Freely; to flow unstained;
And never may rude hand thy music hush
   Till all our glory's gained.

Thy inspirer and thy maker, worthy each,
   The soil from which they sprung—
For brother-love and love of art they teach;
   Pioneers, though so young.

Oh, California, fair as any dream!
   On thee, the world shall wait;
And steadily the nations all shall stream
   Through the wide Golden Gate!

     —September 5, 1897, presented at the
    dedication of the Admission Day Fountain

TILDEN'S MAJOR EXHIBITS
AND DISPLAYS AT EXPOSITIONS

SALON OF THE SOCIETÉ DES ARTISTES FRANCAIS ET SOCIETEÉ NATIONALE DES BEAUX ARTS, PARIS, FRANCE.

1889

The Baseball Player, plaster.

1890

The Baseball Player, bronze.
The Tired Boxer, plaster, Awarded—"Honorable".

1891

The Tired Boxer, bronze.

1892

The Bear Hunt, bronze.
The Young Acrobat, bronze.

1894

The Football Players, plaster.

WORLD'S COLUMBIAN EXPOSITION, CHICAGO, ILLINOIS

May 1—October 31, 1893.

The Baseball Player, plaster.
The Tired Boxer, plaster.
The Young Acrobat, marble, bronze, and gilt base.
The Bear Hunt, bronze.

1900

UNIVERSALLE EXPOSITION, PARIS, FRANCE

The Football Players, plaster.
Awarded—Medaille de Bronze.

1901

PAN-AMERICAN EXPOSITION, BUFFALO, NEW YORK

The Football Players, plaster.

1904

ST. LOUIS EXPOSITION, ST. LOUIS, MISSOURI

Architectural Decoration, Tympanum,
Industries Building.
Awarded—Commemorative Gold Medal

1909

ALASKA-YUKON PACIFIC EXPOSITION
SEATTLE, WASHINGTON

Father Junipero Serra, plaster medallion
Awarded—Gold Medal

Displayed models in numerous exhibitions at the Mark Hopkins Institute of Art,
and in the Bohemian Club Annual, San Francisco.

SELECTED BIBLIOGRAPHY—

BOOKS

Adams, Adeline. *The Spirit of American Sculpture*. New York: Gillis Press, 1923.

Berkeley: The First Seventy-Five Years. Compiled by writer's program of the W.P.A. in Northern California, California State Department of Education, 1941.

Broder, Patricia Janis. *Bronzes of the American West*. New York: Harry N. Abrams, n.d. (1975), pp. 258–259.

Burnes, Caroline H. and Catherine M. Ramger. *A History of the California School for the Deaf, 1860–1960*. Berkeley: printed by the Students, California School for the Deaf, Berkeley, 1960.

California Art Research, Vol. VI. "Robert Aikens." "Earl Cummings." "Douglas Tilden." W.P.A. Project, 1937.

Conmy, Peter Thomas. *The Beginnings of Oakland, California, A.U.C.* Oakland: Oakland Public Library, 1961.

Cornelius, Brother. *Keith, Old Master of California*. Fresno: Academy Library Guild, 1957, II, 293.

Craven, Wayne. *Sculpture in America*. New York: Thomas Y. Crowell, 1968.

Elsen, Albert E. *Rodin*. New York: Museum of Modern Art, 1963.

Ferrier, William Warren. *Berkeley, California: The Story of the Evolution of a Hamlet Into a City of Culture and Commerce*. Published by author, 1933.

Gallagher, James E., ed. *Representative Deaf Persons*. Chicago, 1898, p. 21.

Gardner, Albert Ten Eyck. *American Sculpture: A Catalogue of the Collection of the Metropolitan Museum of Art*. Greenwich, Connecticut: distributed by the New York Graphic Society, 1965.

Godine, David R. *200 Years of American Sculpture*. New York: David R. Godine in association with the Whitney Museum of American Art, 1976.

Goode, James M. *The Outdoor Sculpture of Washington, D.C.: A Comprehensive Historical Guide*. Washington: Smithsonian Institution Press, 1974.

Hale, William Harlan. The World of Rodin. New York: Time-Life Books, 1969.

Hansell, Franz T. *Opinionated Guide to San Francisco*. Sausalito: Comstock Editions, 1973.

Hansen, Gladys. *San Francisco Almanac*. San Francisco: Chronicle Books, 1975.

Hittell, John S. A History of the City of San Francisco and Incidentally of the State of California. San Francisco: A. L. Bancroft, 1878.

Hoover, Mildred Brooke; Hero Eugene Rensch; and Ethel Grace Rensch. *Historic Spots in California,* third edition. Stanford: Stanford University Press, 1968.

Howard, Eric. "Douglas Tilden," *in* Rockwell D. Hunt, ed. *California and Californians*. Chicago: Lewis Publishing Company, 1926, III, 133.

Jackson, Joseph Henry, ed. *The Western Gate*. New York: Farrar, Straus & Young, 1952. pp. 263–264.

Johnson, Rossiter, ed. *The History of the World Columbian Exposition*. New York: Appleton, 1897, 1898, III, 409.

Johstone, Parker Lochiel. *Mission-Presidio Diary, San Francisco, 1776*. San Francisco: published by the author, 1970.

Kaucher, Dorothy. *James D. Phelan, a Portrait*. Saratoga: Gallery Committee of Montalvo Association, Saratoga, 1965.

Mandall, Richard D. *Paris 1900: The Great World's Fair*. Toronto: University of Toronto Press, 1967.

Millard, Bailey. *History of the San Francisco Bay Region*. San Francisco: The American Historical Society, 1924.

Neville, Amelia Ransome. *The Fantastic City*. New York: Houghton & Miflin, 1932.

Reed, Herbert. *A Concise History of Modern Sculpture*. New York: Praeger, 1965.

Reed, Merrill, A. *Historical Statues & Monuments in California*. Burlingame: Burlingame Press, 1956.

Beautiful Santa Cruz County. Santa Cruz, 1896.

Sibley, Robert and Carol. University of California Pilgrimage: *A Treasury of Tradition, Lore and Laughter*. Berkeley: printed by Lederer, Street, & Zeus, 1957.

Snipper, Martin, ed. *A Survey of Art Work in the City and County of San Francisco*. San Francisco: published by the Office of Mayor Joseph L. Alioto, 1975.

Starr, Kevin. *Americans and the California Dream*. New York: Oxford University Press, 1973.

Taft, Loredo. *History of American Sculpture*. New York: MacMillan, 1903.

Tharp, Louise Hall. *Saint-Gaudens and the Gilded Era*. Boston: Little, Brown, 1969.

Thorp, Margaret Farrand. *The Literary Sculptors*. Durham, North Carolina: Duke University Press, 1965.

Walker, Franklin. *San Francisco's Literary Frontier*. New York: Knopf, 1939.

Van Nostrand, Jeanne. *Monterey, Adobe Capital of California. 1770–1847*. San Francisco: California Historical Society, 1968.

PERIODICALS

Albronda, Mildred. "Tilden's Admission Day Statue Returns to Market Street." *The California News* (California School for the Deaf, Berkeley), (April-May, 1977.)

Armes, William Dallum. "Douglas Tilden, Sculptor." *Overland Monthly* (February, 1898), pp. 142–153.

Bland, Henry Meade. "Two Representative Men of California, Benjamin Ide Wheeler and Douglas Tilden." *Overland Monthly* (November, 1906), pp. 329–336.

Brown, Joseph E. "Sentinels of the Western Shore." *Westways* (June, 1974).

Dake, Callista. "Douglas Tilden, the Mute Sculptor." *News & Notes from the Santa Cruz Historical Society* (June, 1965). Pamphlet no. 31.

"Deaf Artists and Sculptors." *The Silent Worker,* X, no. 5 (January, 1898, pp. 5–6.

D'Estrella, Theophilus Hope. "The Itemizer." Column in the *California News* (from 1885 to 1929). Numerous articles, letters from, tidbits about Douglas Tilden.

Hall, Kate Montague. "The Mark Hopkins Institute of Art—A Department of the University of California." *Overland Monthly* XXX (July-December, 1897), pp. 539–548.

Parisina (pseudonym). "The Silent Sculptor." *The Argonaut* (June 8, 1892).

Ruckstall, F. W. "World War Monuments." *Art World* (January, 1919), p. 127.

Runde, W. S. "Douglas Tilden, Sculptor." *The Silent Worker* (December, 1952), pp. 3–5.

Stackpole, Ralph. "Decorative Sculpture in California." *Pacific Coast Architect* XIII (January-June, 1917), p. 53.

"The Sculpture of Douglas Tilden." *The Silent Worker.* XVI:3 (December, 1903), pp. 33–44. 25 illustrations.

"Douglas Tilden." *The Silent Worker.* VII:2 (October, 1894), pp. 1–4.

"Douglas Tilden: Deaf Sculptor." *The Digest of the Deaf.* II:4 (January, 1940), pp. 14–19.

Tilden, Douglas. "Deaf Mutes and Their Education." *Overland Monthly* (May, 1885), pp. 504–510.

_____ . "Articultaion in the New Light." *American Annals of the Deaf.* XXXII (1887), pp. 98–103.

_____ .(pseudonym Clarence Stairly). "The Artist's Testament." Short story. *Overland Monthly* (April, 1888), pp. 395–402.

_____ . "Paris." *Deaf Mutes Journal* (December, 27, 1888).

_____ . "Art Among the Deaf in France." *American Annals of the Deaf.* XXXIV, p. 30.

_____ . "Notes of an Idle Morning." *The Weekly News* (of the California School for the Deaf, Berkeley), (November 23, 1889).

_____ . "What is the Object of Art Instruction?" *The Silent Educator* (Michigan School for the Deaf), (January, 1891), p. 247.

_____ . "Higher Education of the Deaf." Prepared for the British Congress of the Deaf held in Glasgow, Scotland, August 3, 1891. *The Silent Educator* (November, 1891), pp. 449–450.

_____ . (pseudonym Zeno). "Half Hour Exercises for the Deaf or a List of Commonest Mistakes in Deaf-Mute Composition." *The Silent Educator* (February, 1891 to May, 1892). Series of ten articles.

_____ . "Art, and What California Should Do About Her." *Overland Monthly* (May, 1892), pp. 509–515.

_____ . "Art Education of the Deaf." A paper prepared for the World's Congress for the Deaf, Chicago, 1893. Exerpts in "Douglas Tilden," *The Silent Worker* (October, 1894).

_____ . "The Poverty of Fortune." First Prize fiction story for contest in *Overland Monthly* (March, 1895), pp. 195–205.

_____ . "Douglas Tilden's Design for the Grant Memorial." *The Silent Worker* (December, 1903), pp. 37–39.

_____ . "Zenoisms." *The Deaf-Mutes Journal* (February 23, March 23, May 11, June 15, and October 5, 1905).

_____ . "The Value of Art to the Deaf." Program of the Twenty-First Meeting of the Convention of American Instructors of the Deaf, American School for the Deaf, Hartford, Connecticut, June 29-July 3, 1917, 85–90.

_____ . "California and Theophilus d'Estrella." *The California News* (November, 1929), pp. 58–59.

Tompkins, Elizabeth K. "A California Sculptor." *Munsey's Magazine* (September, 1898), pp. 914–916.

Wilkinson, Warring J. "Our Art Possibilities." *Overland Monthly* (March, 1869), pp. 248–254.

NEWSPAPERS

I have found more than one hundred newspaper articles about Douglas Tilden, his controversies, and his monumental bronze sculpture. Listed below, in chronological order, is a representative sample of such articles:

The Daily Examiner. San Francisco, January 2, 1889, 5. "The Young Douglas Tilden."

San Francisco Morning Call. Joaquin Miller, "A California Sculptor: Douglas Tilden and his Work." Sunday, October 16, 1892.

San Francisco Chronicle. May 16, 1901. "Crowds Watch Unveiling of Donohue [Mechanics] Fountain."

The Sunday Call, San Francisco. Douglas Tilden, "Deaf Mutes and the World of Pantomime" (full page, illustrated). March 30, 1903.

San Francisco Chronicle. May 14, 1903. "Roosevelt Dedicates Ground to Martyred Predecessor—Pioneers, Veterans and the Native Sons and Daughters of the Golden West Present a Costly Souvenir of Visit."

The Morning Oregonian. May 31, 1906. "Memorial Statue Stands Unveiled."

San Francisco Chronicle. August 13, 1906. "Monument to the California Volunteers is Unveiled with Fitting Ceremonies."

Los Angeles Daily Times. December 12, 1908. "Laurels of Great Love Placed on Beautiful White Memorial."

San Francisco Chronicle. March 8, 1918. "Art Studio given up by Tilden."

San Francisco Chronicle. January 12, 1920. "Douglas Tilden Gives up Art to be Machinist" (frontpage).

San Francisco Call. Eric Howard, "Famous Californians." January 24, 1923, 14.

San Francisco Call. September 12, 1925. George West, "Noted Artist Rises Anew After 20 Years" (front page).

San Francisco Chronicle. June 5, 1930. "Tilden Hurls Forth His Challenge to Modernists."

The New York Times. August 8, 1935. "Douglas Tilden, 75, Sculptor, is Dead."

San Francisco Chronicle. December 10, 1948. Kevin Wallace, "Statue on the Move—The Lady of Turk and Mason is Transplanted." (Front page lead article.)

San Francisco Chronicle. March 1, March 3, and March 6, 1950. Robert O'Brien, Donahue [Mechanics] Monument.

San Francisco Chronicle. January 6, 1977. Chapin A. Day III, "A Monument Returns to Market Street."

San Francisco Sunday Examiner and Chronicle. May 21, 1978. Michael Bower, "A Sculptor in the Heroic Mold." (California Living Section) p. 42.

APPENDIX—PHOTO CREDITS

Pages	Title, Date, Medium, Dimension, Collection	Photographer
113	*Douglas Tilden—Sculptor*. Circa 1895. *Men of the State of California*, Pacific Art Commission, 1901. San Francisco Archives.	—————
114	*Tilden Studying Anatomy*, Cooper Medical College, San Francisco. Circa 1886. Archives, California School for the Deaf, Berkeley.	T. H. d'Estrella (album)
114	*Study after Dante's Inferno*. 1886. Plaster, size not known. Whereabouts of model unknown. Archives, California School for the Deaf.	T. H. d'Estrella (album)
115	*Tilden as quarterback, school football team*. 1886. Archives, California School for the Deaf.	—————
115	*The Tired Wrestler*. Circa 1885. Plaster, 8–9 inches high. Whereabouts unknown. Archives, California School for the Deaf.	T. H. d'Estrella (album)
115	*Tilden's first studio*. Circa 1887. Archives, California School for the Deaf.	T. H. d'Estrella (album)
116	*Tilden's grandmother, Mrs. Margaret Hecox*. Circa 1885–87. Plaster, Size not known. Destroyed in a fire, 1969.	T. H. d'Estrella (album)
116	*Mr. Henry Frank*. Circa 1885–87. Plaster, Size not known. Whereabouts unknown. Archives, California School for the Deaf.	T. H. d'Estrella (album)
116	*Mrs. Pomeroy B. Clark*. Circa 1885–87. Plaster, size unknown. Whereabouts unknown. Archives, California School for the Deaf.	T. H. d'Estrella (album)
117	*Mrs. Pomeroy B. Clark*. Circa 1885–87. Plaster, size not known. Whereabouts unknown. Archives, California School for the Deaf.	T. H. d'Estrella (album)
117	*Poetry*. Circa 1885–87. Plaster, bas-relief, size not known, medallion. Whereabouts unknown. Archives, California School for the Deaf.	T. H. d'Estrella (album)
117	*Self-Portrait, Tilden*. Circa 1885–87. Plaster, bas-relief, medallion. Whereabouts unknown. Archives, California School for the Deaf.	T. H. d'Estrella (album)
118	*The Young Acrobat*. 1891–92. Plaster, size not known. Photograph, *Overland Monthly*, February, 1898. Dimensions and present location unknown.	Photocopy, Peter Palmquist
118	*The Baseball Player*. 1888–89. Plaster cast, life-size. Whereabouts unknown. *Overland Monthly*, February, 1898.	Photocopy, Peter Palmquist
118	*The Bear Hunt*. 1891–1892. Plaster cast, 9 feet high. Disposed of in Paris, 1894. Photograph, Archives, California School for the Deaf.	—————
119	*The Tired Boxer*. 1890. Plaster cast, life-size. Disposed of in Chicago circa 1922. Reprint, *Overland Monthly*, February, 1898.	—————
119	*The Football Players*. 1893. Plaster cast, over-life size. Whereabouts unknown. Photograph, *Overland Monthly*, February, 1898.	Photocopy, Peter Palmquist
120	*Mark Hopkins Institute of Art*. Nob Hill, San Francisco. A department of the University of California, Berkeley, circa 1897. Courtesy California Historical Society, San Francisco.	Taber

120   *Professor Tilden and the Boy's Modeling class at the Mark Hopkins Institute of Art, 1897.* Photocopy, reprint, *Overland Monthly,* July-December, 1897, p. 540.   —————

121   Willis Polk, *Architectural Drawing of Tilden's Admission Day Monument.* Circa 1895. Archives, California School for the Deaf.   Photocopy, Peter Palmquist

122   *Mechanics monument and fountain dedication ceremony, May 15, 1901.* Original photograph, Archives, California School for the Deaf.   —————

124   *Tilden's studio in carriage house of residence, Oakland, 1902–1918.* Archives, California School for the Deaf.   T. H. d'Estrella (album)

124   *Tilden's Victorian home, 1545 Webster Street, Oakland, California.* Archives, California School for the Deaf.   T. H. d'Estrella (album)

124   *Daughter Gladys, baby, and wife Bessie, 1903.* Archives, California School for the Deaf.   T. H. d'Estrella (album)

125   *Tilden's "The Poverty of Fortune," First Prize Story. Overland Monthly,* March 1898.   Photocopy, Peter Palmquist

126   *Plaster model, architectural decoration.* Circa 1902. For pediment of Building of Industries, St. Louis Louisiana Purchase Exposition, 1904. Whereabouts unknown. Archives, California School for the Deaf.   T. H. d'Estrella (album)

126   *Joseph LeConte, Professor of Geology, University of California, Berkeley.* 1905. Bronze tablet, fireplace, Le Conte Lodge, Yosemite Valley. Photograph 1979.   Peter Palmquist

126   *William Keith, landscape painter.* 1931. Plaster portrait mask, over-life size. Saint Mary's College, Moraga, California.   Mildred Albronda (transparency)

127   *Tilden's charcoal drawing, "Boy with the Rake."* n.d., 6½ × 5½ inches. E. B. Crocker Art Gallery, Sacramento, California.   —————

128   *Clay or plaster model of California Volunteers.* Circa 1903, 2–3 feet high, front view. Archives, California School for the Deaf.   T. H. d'Estrella (album)

128   *Clay or plaster model of California Volunteers.* Circa 1903, 2–3 feet high, rear view. Archives, California School for the Deaf.   T. H. d'Estrella (album)

128   *Final plaster model of California Volunteers.* Circa 1903–05, 12 feet high. Archives, California School for the Deaf.   T. H. d'Estrella (album)

129   *Tilden working on final clay model, California Volunteers.* Circa 1903–05. Archives, California School for the Deaf.   T. H. d'Estrella (album)

129   *Tilden building up final clay model on armature. California Volunteers.* Circa 1903–05. Archives, California School for the Deaf.   T. H. d'Estrella (album)

130   *San Francisco—Donohue [Mechanics] Fountain,* May 19, 1906. Postcard. San Francisco Archives.   Photocopy, Peter Palmquist

130   *In Honor of California Volunteers—Erected Since the Fire.* Postcard. San Francisco Archives.   Photocopy, Peter Palmquist

131   *The Ruins of San Francisco, after the earthquake and fire, April 18, 1906. "In a nutshell."* Postcard. San Francisco Archives.   Photocopy, Peter Palmquist

131   *Destruction of San Francisco by fire, April 18, 1906.* Postcard. San Francisco Archives.   Photocopy, Peter Palmquist

132   *Golden Gate.* Plaster, 1907; bronze cast, 1969; 16½ inches high.   —————
        Inscription: To Mr. and Mrs. Jack London, November 12, 1916.
        Collection of The Oakland Museum, gift of Mr. and Mrs. Robert
        Neuhaus.

132   *Bear Hunt.* 1903. California gold—paper weight form, 8 inches high.   (transparency)
        Inscription: To President Roosevelt from the Society of California
        Pioneers, the Native sons of the Golden West, and the Native
        Daughters of the Golden West. San Francisco, California, May
        13, 1903. Collection of Old Orchard Museum, Sagamore Hill
        National Historic Site, Oyster Bay, New York.

132   *Oregon Volunteers.* 1904–05. Bronze figure, 7 feet high, atop a   —————
        granite shaft and base, 25 feet high. Dedicated May 30, 1906, Plaza
        Park, Portland, Oregon. Oregon Historical Society.

133   *Grief.* Valentine family memorial monument. Circa late 1890s.   T. H. d'Estrella
        Bronze, 8–9 feet high. Situated in Cypress Lawn Memorial Park   (album)
        Cemetery, Colma, California.

133   *Senator Stephen M. White.* Circa 1905–1907. Bronze, over-life size.   Mildred Albronda
        Situated in front of the Los Angeles Law Library, Los Angeles,   (transparency)
        California. Photograph 1975.

134   *Douglas Tilden, writer Jack London, and painter Granville Seymour*   —————
        Redmond. Circa 1913–1916. Archives, California School for the
        Deaf.

134   *The Fall of Ug* Tilden's gigantic fabricated figure for the Bohemian   —————
        Club's Annual Grove Play by the same name, 1913. Bohemian
        Club, San Francisco.

135   *Tilden in his Berkeley studio, 1934.* Archives, California School for   —————
        the Deaf.

135   *Tilden's plaster model, The Bridge, in his studio, 1934.* Archives,   —————
        California School for the Deaf.

136   *Father Junipero Serra.* Circa 1905–1907. Bronze, 9½ feet high, on   Peter Palmquist
        base 12 feet high. Photograph 1979.

137   *Father Junipero Serra.* Circa 1905–1906. Bronze, 15 inches   Peter Palmquist
        diameter. Historical Museum, Mission Dolores, San Francisco.
        Photograph 1979.

137   *Junipero Serra, 1770.* Tilden designed the medallion for the Celtic   Mildred Albronda
        cross commemorating the landing spot, June 3, 1770, of Father   (transparency)
        Serra. Historical Landmark #128, Monterey, California.

138   *Football Players.* 1893. Bronze, over-life size. Situated near the   Peter Palmquist
        southwest corner, Life Science Building, University of California,
        Berkeley, California. Photograph 1979.

138   *Football Players.* 1893. Bronze, over-life size. Situated near the   Peter Palmquist
        southwest corner, Life Science Building, University of California,
        Berkeley, California. Photograph 1979.

139   *Bear Hunt.* 1891–1892. Bronze, 9 feet high. Courtyard, California   Peter Palmquist
        School for the Deaf. Photograph 1979.

140   *Twelve Stages of Man.* Circa 1910–1912. Tilden created twelve   Peter Rockwell
        bronze bas-relief insets for the outer edge of the Georgian marble   (transparency)

pool of the John E. McElroy Memorial Fountain, Lakeside Park, Oakland, California. Photograph 1976.

140   *One of the Twelve Stages of Man.* Above; bronze, bas-relief inset. Photograph 1979.   Peter Palmquist

141   *Baseball Player.* 1888–1889. Bronze, life-size. Situated in Golden Gate Park, San Francisco. Photograph 1979.   Peter Palmquist

142   *California Volunteers.* 1903–1906. Bronze, 12 feet high atop 10 feet high granite base. Situated at Market and Dolores streets, San Francisco. Photograph 1979.   Peter Palmquist

143   *Mechanics.* Circa 1898–1903. Bronze, 15 feet high atop 6½ feet high granite base. Situated at Market, Battery, and Bush streets, San Francisco. Photograph 1979.   Peter Palmquist

144   *Admission Day.* 1895–1897. Bronze, over-life figures. Total monument, 35 feet high. Situated at Market, Post, and Montgomery streets, San Francisco. Photograph 1979.   Peter Palmquist

INDEX

DOUGLAS TILDEN
SCULPTOR

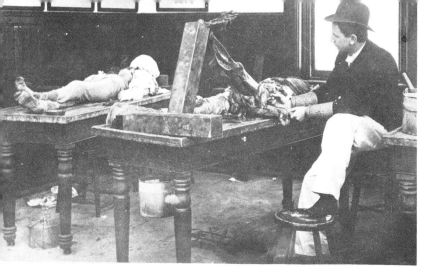

Tilden studying anatomy, Cooper Medical College, San Francisco, circa 1885.

Plaster model created after studying Dante's *Inferno* for two years. Signed, Douglas Tilden, Sculptor, '86.

Tilden, top row center, as quarterback on school's football team (faculty and students), 1886. Tilden had a passion for sports.

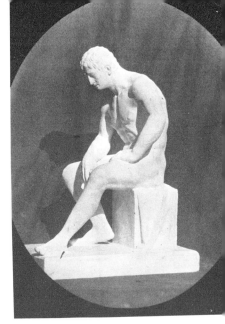

The Tired Wrestler, plaster, 8-9 inches high. First finished model.

First studio, in an old laundry shed, at the California School for the Deaf, Berkeley, circa 1887.

115

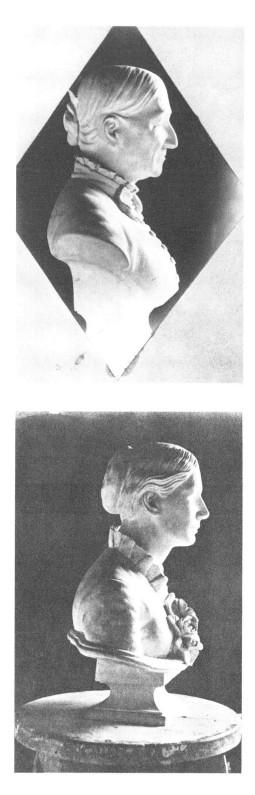

HEADS, 1885-1886. Dimensions and whereabouts unknown.

Upper left: *Mrs. Margaret Hecox*, Tilden's grandmother, plaster.

Upper right: *Mr. Frank*, plaster. First bust attempted.

Lower: *Mrs. Pomeroy Clark*, first Director of the California School for the Deaf when it was situated in San Francisco. Plaster.

Opposite, upper: *Mrs. Pomeroy Clark*, plaster.

Opposite, lower left: *Poetry*, plaster, bas-relief, medallion.

Opposite, lower right: *Self-portrait*, plaster, bas-relief, medallion.

TILDEN EXHIBITS IN THE SALON
Societe Des Artistes Francais et Societe Nationale des Beaux-Arts

For the sculptor, having his work accepted in the Salon was the hallmark of success, leading to fame and fortune, and the sought after commissions for civic monuments. The Salons of sculpture were almost a sea of white plaster—the bronze casting came later when the artist could afford it.

The Young Acrobat. Plaster, size not known. Exhibited: Salon, 1892.

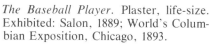

The Baseball Player. Plaster, life-size. Exhibited: Salon, 1889; World's Columbian Exposition, Chicago, 1893.

The Bear Hunt. Plaster, 9 feet high. Exhibited: Salon, 1892. Chicago Exposition, 1893.

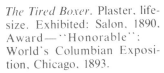

he Football Players. Plaster, over-life ze. Exhibited: Salon, 1894; Paris Exosition, 1900—Bronze medal; Pannerican Exposition, Buffalo, New ork, 1901.

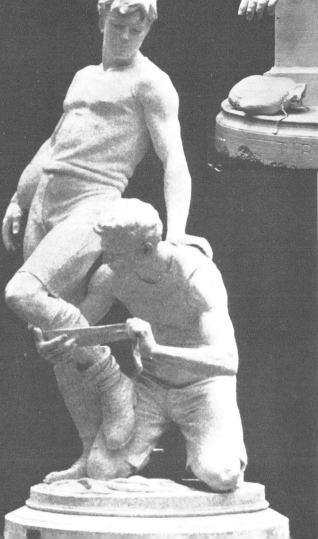

The Tired Boxer. Plaster, life-size. Exhibited: Salon, 1890, Award—``Honorable``; World's Columbian Exposition, Chicago, 1893.

Mark Hopkins Institute of Art, Nob Hill, San Francisco. A department of the University of California, Berkeley, circa 1897.

Professor Tilden and the Boy's Modeling class at the Mark Hopkins Institute of Art, 1897.

Admission Day monument commemorating California's admission to the United States, September 9, 1850. *Architectural drawing* by Willis Polk, architect, who designed the base and pedestal. Tilden's first commission from Mayor James Duval Phelan for the planned Renaissance of San Francisco, 1895. See poem, "The Unveiling of the Fountain," p. 89.

Mechanics monument and fountain. Bronze. Dedication ceremonies, May 15, 1901. Market, Bush, and Battery streets, San Francisco. President William McKinley scheduled to attend.

Tilden's studio, Oakland, 1902-1918.

Tilden's Victorian home, 1545 Webster Street, Oakland.

Daughter Gladys, new baby, and wi[
Bessie, 1903.

Overland Monthly

VOL. XXXI. (Second Series.) — March, 1898.— No. 183

First Prize, story, "The Poverty of Fortune," *Overland Monthly*, March, 1898.

PRIZE · STORY ·
THE · POVERTY · OF
FORTVNE · FIRST ·
PRIZE ·
BY · DOVGLAS · TILDEN ·

R·I·AITKEN

T EXACTLY half past four Harry Treadwell filled and lighted his pipe and kicked the rattan lounge into position in front of the statue.

Just then the door of the studio opened and shut briskly.

"Hello, Dick!" cried Treadwell. "It must go on record that you keep your appointment for the first time in your life. But, Dick, for heaven's sake, do not ask me to do anything on your bust today for I am dead tired. I have just finished the statue."

A curtain in one corner of the room parted, and out came an ancient dame, her palsied hands still busied with the buttons of her dress.

"Good day, sir," mumbled she. "Have you any further use for me?"

"No, thank you," replied the young sculptor cheerily. "Come around again in— ahem!— say a week, and I will pay you. Goodby, model."

He was in a pleasant mood. Before his half-closed eyes was a mass of wet gray clay that he had during eight months, manipulated

Architectural decoration. Plaster model, pediment, front elevation of the Building of Industries, St. Louis Louisiana Purchase Exposition, 1904. Awarded: *Commemorative Gold Medal.*

William Keith. Over-life size, plaster portrait mask, 1931. Created for the opening of the William Keith Gallery, St. Mary's College, Moraga, California.

Joseph Le Conte, Professor of Geology, University of California, Berkeley, and Sierra Club member. Memorial tablet for Le Conte Lodge, Yosemite Valley.

The Boy with the Rake. Tilden's charcoal-drawing, 6½ × 5½ inches. Collection, E.B. Crocker Art Gallery, Sacramento, California.

Photo A—Clay or plaster model, *California Volunteers*, 2-3 feet high, front view.

B—Clay or plaster model, *California Volunteers*, 2-3 feet high, rear view.

CREATING A TILDEN MONUMENT
CALIFORNIA VOLUNTEERS, 1902-05

Photos A and B: Tilden first made several small clay models to achieve his composition and proportions.

Photos D and E: Next, a six-foot, or larger, clay model was built up on a turning table with iron supports (armature). This clay model was kept moist at all times with wet cloths—a task that took several months. Here Tilden added the final touches that gave his creation its "beauty, charm, poetry, and fire."

Photo C: The final plaster cast ready for the fondeur and the final bronze casting. A monumental work took Tilden two or three years to complete and cost approximately $20,000.

C—Final plaster model, *California Volunteers* 12 feet high. Ready for the bronze casting.

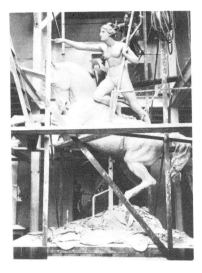

D—Tilden working on final clay model, *California Volunteers*.

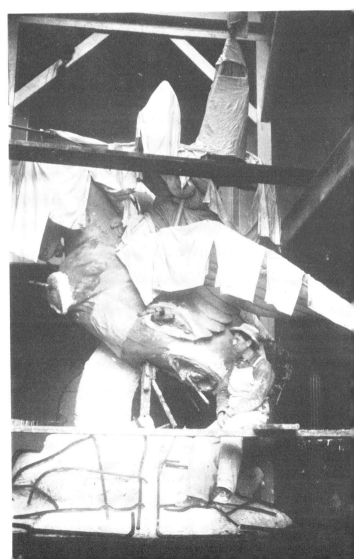

—Tilden building up final clay model on armature; wet cloths necessary to keep clay moist.

POSTCARD MEMENTOS, 1906

San Francisco, Cal.

Donahue Fountain
May 19 th 1906

DEDICATED TO MECHANICS
BY JAMES MERVYN DONAHUE
IN MEMORY OF HIS FATHER
PETER DONAHUE

In Honor of California Volunteers—Erected Since the Fire.

DESTRUCTION OF SAN FRANCISCO BY FIRE, APRIL 18, 1906

"fire and earthquake fiends did not destroy
. . . . Forever evidence that it is the fate
of art to be immortal."

Golden Gate. Plaster, 1907; bronze, 1969; 16½ inches high. Inscription: To Mr. and Mrs. Jack London, November 12, 1916. Collection of The Oakland Museum, gift of Mr. and Mrs. Robert Neuhaus.

Bear Hunt. Replica, California gold, 8 inches high, 1903. Inscription: To President Roosevelt from the Society of California Pioneers, the Native Sons of the Golden West, and the Native Daughters of the Golden West. San Francisco, California, May 13, 1903. Collection: of Old Orchard Museum, Sagamore Hill National Historic Site, Oyster Bay, New York.

Oregon Volunteers. Bronze figure, 7 feet high, atop a granite shaft and base, 25 feet high. Ernest Coxhead, architect, designed the base and shaft. Situated in Plaza Park, Portland, Oregon. Dedicated May 30, 1906.

Grief. Valentine family memorial monument. Bronze, 8-9 feet high, circa late 1890s. Cypress Lawn Memorial Park Cemetery, Colma, California.

Senator Stephen M. White. Bronze, over-life size. Situated in front of the Los Angeles Law Library, Los Angeles, California. Dedicated December 11, 1908.

Douglas Tilden, writer Jack London, and painter Granville Redmond. Circa 1913-1916. Bohemian Club Pals.

The Fall of Ug. Tilden's gigantic fabricated figure for Bohemian Club's Annual Grove Play, 1913.

Tilden in his Berkeley studio, 1934.

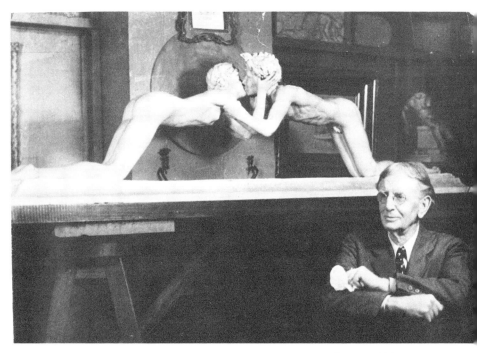

The Bridge. Plaster model in Tilden's studio, Berkeley, 1934.

135

Father Junipero Serra. Bronze, 9½ feet high, on base 12 feet high. Edgar Matthews, architect, designed the base. A wreath is placed on the monument in Golden Gate Park each June 29 to celebrate the birthday of San Francisco. The traditional ceremony is performed by the Native Daughters of the Golden West and the Native Sons of the Golden West to whom this monument was originally dedicated, November 17, 1907.

Father Junipero Serra. Bronze medallion, 15 inches diameter. Historical Museum. Mission Dolores, San Francisco.

Junipero Serra, 1770. Historical Landmark, #128, Monterey, California. Tilden designed the medalion left for the Celtic cross commemorating the landing spot of Father Serra at Monterey, June 3, 1770. Granite, 12 feet high. Architect unknown.

Football Players. Bronze, over-life size (close-up).

Football Players. Bronze, over-life size. University of California, Berkeley. Southwest corner Life Science Building. Dedicated May 12, 1900.

138

Bear Hunt. Bronze, 9 feet high. Courtyard, California School for the Deaf, Berkeley.
Placed 1895.

Twelve Stages of Man. Tilden created twelve bronze bas-relief insets for the outer edge of the Georgian marble pool of the John E. McElroy Memorial Fountain, Lakeside Park, Oakland, California.

One of the *Twelve Stages of Man.* Bronze, bas-relief inset.

Baseball Player. Bronze, life-size. John Wright, architect. Inscription: Presented by a close friend [Mr. W.E. Brown] of the sculptor as a tribute to his energy, industry, and ability. Dedicated July 8, 1891, Golden Gate Park, San Francisco.

California Volunteers. Bronze, 12 feet high atop 10 feet high granite base. Architect not known. Dedicated August 12, 1906, Market and Van Ness, as the first new monument placed for Market Street redevelopment after the earthquake and fire.

DEDICATED TO MECHANICS
BY JAMES MERVYN DONAHUE
IN MEMORY OF HIS FATHER
PETER DONAHUE

Mechanics. Bronze, 15 feet high atop 6½ feet high granite base. Willis Polk, architect, designed the base. Dedicated May 15, 1903, Market, Battery, and Bush streets.

Admission Day. Detail, bronze over-life size figure. Total monument 35 feet high.
Commemorates the admission of California into the United States September 9, 1850.
Dedicated September 5, 1897, Mason, Turk, and Markets streets.
Moved to Golden Gate Park, December 1948. Returned to Market, Post, and
Montgomery streets, January, 1977. Rededicated as part of Market Street Redevel-
opment Project April 27, 1977 by Mayor George Moscone.